GRACE

IN THE BOOK OF ROMANS

MIKE MAZZALONGO

BibleTalk.TV

"God's grace brought Jesus to earth to die for our sins. This is the fundamental story of the Bible. Paul, the Apostle, beautifully encapsulates this story of God's grace in his epistle to the Romans where he teaches that "all are justified freely by his grace through the redemption that came by Christ" (Romans 3:24). In his book, Grace in the Book of Romans, Mike Mazzalongo insightfully traces the gospel of grace as Paul develops it throughout the epistle. Mike's book shows how Paul presents the need for grace, the response to grace and the final outcome of grace. Brother Mazzalongo's work provides a deeper understanding of both the book of Romans and the important topic of grace.

Stafford North
Late Distinguished Professor of Bible
Oklahoma Christian University

Paperback ISBN: 9781945778964
Hardcover ISBN: 9798852909442

BibleTalk.tv
14998 E. Reno
Choctaw, Oklahoma 73020

Research Commentary:
Commentary on the New Testament
R.C.H. Lenski

TABLE OF CONTENTS

1. Introduction

The book of Romans contains some of the most challenging ideas in the entire Bible. Many have called this epistle Paul's Ph.D. thesis on Christianity. The book fits this description because in it Paul examines the core ideas of the Christian faith and answers many questions posed by both skeptics and believers concerning the gospel. Let us begin, therefore, by looking at a passage that summarizes the entire epistle.

THE GOSPEL OF GRACE

Many scholars point to Romans 1:16 as the key verse in Romans because it distills into one sentence the whole point of not only the book of Romans, but the entire Bible itself.

> For I am not ashamed of the gospel, for it is the power of God for salvation to everyone who believes, to the Jew first and also to the Greek.
> - Romans 1:16

When a person actually reads through the Bible, and the book of Romans in particular, they discover that yes, the gospel is God's power to save man, but the power that the gospel has is that through it the grace of God is revealed. This is why any time the gospel is preached and the main point made is something other than the grace of God revealed to men through Christ, the main point has been missed. For example, if the main point being made is that baptism is by immersion, or that there is only one church, or that the Bible is inspired etc., you have explained certain true principles contained in the Bible but you have not successfully preached the gospel itself.

This is why we often fail to bring people to Christ. We teach them many biblical doctrines but we neglect to expose them to the one thing in the Bible that has the power to save and change a person, and that is the good news (gospel) of God's grace extended to sinful man. Nothing builds one's faith and hope more than a deeper understanding of God's grace, and this is the main goal in the writing of this book.

OUTLINE — GRACE IN ROMANS

The Renouncing of Grace - Romans 1:1-3:20

- The problem of universal sin.
- Paul begins explaining the concept of grace by detailing man's fall from grace and the state of universal sinfulness.
- You cannot understand light if you do not understand darkness. Paul begins with darkness.

The Response of Grace - Romans 3:20-7:25

- The cross of Christ is God's response to man's rejection of His initial offer of grace.

The Request of Grace - Romans 8

- Grace stimulates a response from man that the Law cannot.
- Grace enables man to live a "spirit filled" life.

The Refusal of Grace - Romans 9-11

- Why did the Jewish people stumble?

- Paul uses the Jews as an example of what happens to "religious people" who refuse God's grace.

- In chapters 1 and 2 he talks about those who fall from grace without religion; in chapters 9 to 11 he describes those who fall from grace but do so with all the trappings of religion.

The Result of Grace - Romans 12-16

- The result of grace is the church of Christ.

- Paul describes in detail what grace looks like in the lives of those who experience it.

- In the end, the church is the collective expression of those who are experiencing God's grace.

DEFINITIONS AND MISCONCEPTIONS OF GRACE

Basic Definition

In the Old Testament the idea of grace was often seen as something that would come in the future. Their main thought was that eventually God would have mercy on them and save them from every enemy or sin, this was grace, out there in the future.

In the New Testament the English word "grace" comes from two words in the original Greek; one was the word "charis" which meant favor, and another was the word "eleo" which meant mercy. Grace, in the New Testament, was not seen as an object or event to happen in the future, but rather a disposition or attitude that God had toward man in regards to his failures and sins in the present.

> [4] But when the kindness of God our Savior and His love for mankind appeared, [5] He saved us, not on the basis of deeds which we have done in righteousness, but according to His

> mercy, by the washing of regeneration and renewing by the Holy Spirit, [6] whom He poured out upon us richly through Jesus Christ our Savior, [7] so that being justified by His grace we would be made heirs according to the hope of eternal life.
> - Titus 3:4-7

For the writers of the New Testament, grace begins with God's attitude of love and mercy toward men and is perceived through His concrete actions throughout history. These actions are the outworking of His grace.

Christianity's theology is based on this element of God's character, exalts this expression of His divinity and sees this as the motivating factor in His dealings with mankind. We will develop these ideas as we study Paul's epistle, but for now, suffice to say that grace is both an attitude and a quality of God's character that manifests itself in love and mercy towards sinful man.

MISCONCEPTIONS

There have been some rather serious misconceptions about grace throughout the years. Many of these have resulted in the development of entire religious systems, some of which are still with us today.

Grace - Roman Catholic Church

Catholic teaching says that grace is a spiritual commodity distributed through the "sacraments" delivered through the intermediary work of their clergy. These religious ceremonies (Baptism, Communion, Confirmation, Holy Matrimony, Holy Orders, Penance, Extreme Unction) and the authority of the priest or bishop administering them, infuse these actions with "sanctifying grace" (grace that has salvific power). Catholic teaching also speaks of "actual grace," which is an everyday type of grace. It is experienced at Christmas and other holidays in the liturgical Catholic calendar, and is meant to bring joy and happiness into the life of the Catholic believer but has no power to save.

The Catholic view of grace sees it as an ingredient contained in these rites which, with repetition, supposedly lead to salvation and greater holiness. The sacraments serve as a kind of spiritual supplement for the believer.

In my opinion, this view of grace is incorrect because it uses grace as a commodity to be distributed rather than an attitude of mercy exhibited by God in His relationship with man. The danger of this commodity view is that it leads to legalism in its worst form as the believer strives to be saved and grow in Christ by repeating ceremonies that earn him spiritual favors instead of trusting in God's grace offered to him through the gospel.

Pelagianism

Pelagianism was a fourth century heresy that put onto man the task of saving himself. It taught that with the knowledge of the law and single-minded determination, a person could live a sinless life. Greater knowledge and self-will worked hand in hand towards greater improvement.

Most self-help books work on this same principle: with the right knowledge and will-power you can do anything...Just do it! The Bible, however, teaches the exact opposite. Man is helpless to change or improve himself to the point of salvation. This is what grace is for: to provide salvation to those who recognize that they cannot save themselves.

> For while we were still helpless, at the right time Christ died for the ungodly.
> - Romans 5:6

Calvinism / Predestination / Election

John Calvin's concept of grace taught that God arbitrarily chose some for salvation and condemned others. This meant that an individual was saved or lost, and could do nothing good or bad to reverse this condition.

This idea of grace is incorrect because it eliminates man's responsibility to exercise his free moral agency in the process of his own salvation. That human beings can know and choose to do what is right despite their sinful nature is well documented in Scripture.

> If it is disagreeable in your sight to serve the Lord, choose for yourselves today whom you will serve: whether the gods which your fathers served which were beyond the River, or the gods of the Amorites in whose land you are living; but as for me and my house, we will serve the Lord."
> - Joshua 24:15
>
> 17 But thanks be to God that though you were slaves of sin, you became obedient from the heart to that form of teaching to which you were committed, 18 and having been freed from sin, you became slaves of righteousness.
> - Romans 6:17-18

The Calvinistic view of grace fails to differentiate between what is conditional and what is free. Something can be free but have certain conditions. For example, air is free but we need to breathe it in for it to be useful; a will leaves an estate to its inheritors for free (they cannot buy it) but certain conditions must be met. In the same way grace and its benefits are free and offered freely but they are not without conditions. Conditions do not make something less free. Throughout the Bible God has always placed conditions on man for everything, even salvation, where belief is the primary condition.

Calvinism presents grace as something that God distributes arbitrarily without any conditions since He controls the entire process. He saves those He wills to save and condemns others, all done according to His counsel and without human input. In this system of thought the only ones who receive grace are those God has chosen to save whether they wanted this or not. In doing this, Calvinism removes any joy possible for those who have received salvation in this way.

Legalism

The most common misconception of grace, however, is what I call the "thermometer" explanation of grace. In this imagery the obedience and good works we contribute towards our salvation is represented by the degrees on a thermometer (zero degrees represents zero obedience and good works; 100 degrees represents the amount of obedience and good works necessary to have salvation). In the "thermometer" version of grace the good works and obedience of man are registered first, and whatever is missing in order to reach 100 degrees (necessary for salvation) is added by God. Grace, in this view, is the part that God provides in order to get us to the top. The saying, "God helps those who help themselves" is a good way to summarize this idea of grace. This is classic legalism.

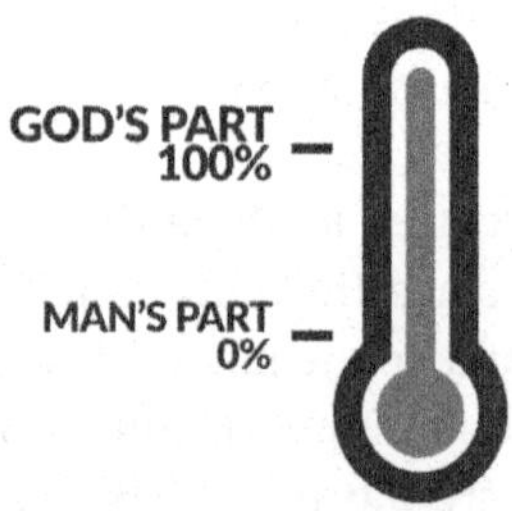

The proper way to use this illustration in describing God's grace is to show that God provides 100% of what is necessary to save man and man provides 0%. This biblical concept says that man does not even possess what is necessary to save himself or others. Not that he might not want to or try to, it is just that he does not have what it takes to accomplish this because salvation cannot be earned with various degrees of human obedience and good works.

According to the Bible, however, man's salvation requires:

- **A perfect life of obedience.** A perfect, sinless life is necessary to avoid condemnation for oneself. In addition to this, a perfect life is also necessary to offer as payment for the moral debt (sins) of others and thus satisfy God's justice. The Bible shows that Jesus is the only person who had the currency necessary to pay the moral debt owed by all men on account of sin.

> 22 who committed no sin, nor was any deceit found in His mouth; 23 and while being reviled, He did not revile in return; while suffering, He uttered no threats, but kept entrusting Himself to Him who judges righteously; 24 and He Himself bore our sins in His body on the cross, so that we might die to sin and live to righteousness; for by His wounds you were healed.
> - I Peter 2:22-24

- **Divine Spirit.** In addition to a perfect life, a divine spirit was also necessary to save mankind because only a divine spirit could enter into the presence of Divinity itself to offer that sacrifice for sin, an entry denied to all men because of their sins and strictly human spiritual nature. It was not enough to live a perfect life, you had to be able to come before God and offer that perfect life. Jesus became a man in order to offer a perfect human life, but He retained His divine nature in order to be able to enter into the presence of Divinity to offer that sacrifice (this is what the book of Hebrews is all about).

> For Christ did not enter a holy place made with hands, a mere copy of the true one, but into heaven itself, now to appear in

> the presence of God for us;
> - Hebrews 9:24
>
> 10 By this will we have been sanctified through the offering of the body of Jesus Christ once for all. 11 Every priest stands daily ministering and offering time after time the same sacrifices, which can never take away sins; 12 but He, having offered one sacrifice for sins for all time, sat down at the right hand of God,
> - Hebrews 10:10-12

GRACE — DEFINITION — SUMMARY

God's original creation of the universe with man at the head of it; His subsequent decision to save fallen man through the method of atonement accomplished by Jesus; His establishment of the church in order to reveal this plan to all mankind. This is the full expression of His favor and mercy, what the Bible refers to as grace.

In the next chapter, we will talk about the original fall from God's first expression of grace, or the universality of sin.

2.
Renouncing of Grace
Part 1

ROMANS 1

The first section of Paul's epistle explains how man has renounced God's initial expression of grace and how this rejection has led to universal sin (Romans 1:1-3:20).

In the opening verses Paul greets his readers and establishes his credentials as an Apostle, he then summarizes the gospel and offers a blessing upon them. He states that his main objective in ministry is to preach the gospel to both Jews and Gentiles, and that the gospel is God's power to save both of these groups since all are guilty of sin.

The Renouncing of Grace

Before we examine Paul's teaching on the universality of sin, we need to look at an opposing view called universality of salvation or by its more modern name, religious pluralism.

Universalism/Pluralism is a popular idea in today's religious world. It says that the love/grace of God ensures that everyone will be saved no matter what path they choose. The main tenets of this view are:

- All religions lead to God.

- Each religion is distinctive because of culture, geography and history, but all are capable of leading a person to God, and thus salvation.

- Some "Christian" pluralists teach that every religion is really a form of undeveloped Christianity that when mature will lead a person to Christ.

Several Christian groups have a similar version of pluralism and teach that all "Christian denominations" lead to heaven (but not all religions).

- These have the same pluralistic ideas but are restricted to Christendom.

- They use the term "religious expression" in referring to other denominations.

Pluralism's ideas are easy to understand and are said to promote religious tolerance, but they have two major flaws:

1. They are illogical

It is illogical to think that God (who is perfectly logical) would give people different and even contradicting information about Himself and how to reach Him. For example, Eastern religions like Hinduism, Jainism and Buddhism do not see God as a unique individual spirit. They also teach that man can reach a state of completeness (nirvana or moksha) and union with the ultimate "life force" either through a cycle of reincarnation and personal effort, or a lifelong quest at acquiring special knowledge and insight through meditation and self-denial.

Here are other contradictory teachings about God from one religion to another: Western religions (Judaism, Christianity, Islam) teach that God is a conscious spirit being who will judge each individual person. Eastern religions see God as a force without personality or will whereas Western religions see Him as sovereign and intelligent. Eastern religions are inclusive, integrating various religious ideas into their belief systems. Western religions are exclusive, requiring adherence to only one religion.

The point here is that the information about Hinduism, for example, will not lead a person to the same God and result as the information about Islam or Christianity. A logical God, therefore, does not purposefully give conflicting information about Himself that, in the end, can only result in confusion.

2. The Bible does not support Universalism/Pluralism

The Bible, and especially the book of Romans, have a decidedly exclusive view of the Christian religion. The Bible assures all Christians that they are positively and completely saved forever, but it also emphatically declares that those who are not Christians will perish (Mark 16:15-16; Acts 4:12).

It is for this reason that the Christian religion was so despised in the beginning. At a time when all religions were inclusive (you could be a collector of gods and religions, the more the better), the Apostles appeared and said, "There is no other name under heaven... by which we must be saved" (Acts 4:12). The disciples of Jesus were not martyred because Christianity was a new or different religion, they were persecuted because they dared to say that theirs was the only religion of the true God and all others were to be rejected.

In his letter to the Romans, Paul explains why this is so.

THE FALL FROM GRACE

Paul begins his message to the church in Rome by teaching them that mankind has fallen from God's grace and is in a state of universal sin. He explains that man began as good and was the recipient of God's grace in that he was placed at the head of creation, partook of the divine nature and was permitted to have an intimate relationship with God. This was God's initial expression of grace towards man. Through disobedience, however, man fell from or renounced this grace resulting in the condition (universal sin and lostness) that Paul outlines in the first three chapters of his letter.

He describes this fall by illustrating the process of sin itself and how it leads to judgment and death.

> For the wrath of God is revealed from heaven against all ungodliness and unrighteousness of men who suppress the truth in unrighteousness,
> - Romans 1:18

God punishes all those who refuse to accept and willingly suppress the truth (i.e. the truth that there is a God; that He can be known; that He is to be obeyed). This truth has such great evidentiary power that it has to be willfully suppressed in order to be denied.

> 19 because that which is known about God is evident within them; for God made it evident to them. 20 For since the creation of the world His invisible attributes, His eternal power and divine nature, have been clearly seen, being understood through what has been made, so that they are without excuse.
> - Romans 1:19-20

God/truth can be known in two natural ways: through a person's conscience and from the witness of the creation. Paul claims that every person can come to know God and His attributes through either or both of these means, and he concludes that they are so overpowering, no one can plead ignorance.

> 21 For even though they knew God, they did not honor Him as God or give thanks, but they became futile in their speculations, and their foolish heart was darkened.
> 22 Professing to be wise, they became fools, 23 and exchanged the glory of the incorruptible God for an image in the form of corruptible man and of birds and four-footed animals and

> crawling creatures.
> - Romans 1:21-23

Paul charges that instead of responding to a fundamental truth that he has always known, man has willfully chosen to ignore, refuse to honor or be grateful to God. This failing has naturally led man to the worship of baser things expressed in pagan religions, seeing in these a wisdom devised from his own mind. Paul finishes here by saying that instead of letting the truth emerge, man chose to pursue a course that would lead to his eventual destruction.

> 24 Therefore God gave them over in the lusts of their hearts to impurity, so that their bodies would be dishonored among them. 25 For they exchanged the truth of God for a lie, and worshiped and served the creature rather than the Creator, who is blessed forever. Amen.
> - Romans 1:24-25

Paul explains that God did not forcibly stop man from sinning, but instead permitted him to sin to his heart's content. In the final verses, he then details some of the sins that this fall from grace eventually led to.

The Apostle is not describing a single person or nation here but the natural progression of a humanity that forsakes God. This progression includes:

- A refusal to acknowledge God.
- A refusal to respond to God with faith and thanksgiving.
- The subsequent creation of gods devised by humans in order to fulfill the human soul's need for the true God.

DOWNWARD PLUNGE INTO ACTIVE EVIL

From a macrocosmic view of history, the devolution of sinful man proceeds as follows:

- **A state of grace** - man is created without sin, as head of creation living in harmony with God and the creation.

- **A theological fall** - man disobeys God and, as a result, his knowledge and relationship with God are compromised.

- **A philosophical fall** - man fulfills his need for knowledge and God with ideas and gods of his own making.

- **A moral fall** - man changes the original moral order imposed on him by God replacing it with one of his own design.

This process is cyclical in nature as mankind goes from one stage of devolution to another until God interrupts the cycle with a period of renewal and revival through the power of His Word, Spirit and church. God has done this throughout history in order to prevent the total corruption and destruction of mankind similar to events in the world that preceded the great worldwide flood (Genesis 6:5).

The purpose of these interventions by God is to preserve man until both the first and second coming of Christ can occur. The first coming, to allow Jesus to complete His saving work on the cross. The second coming will be His return at the end of the world to judge all men and usher in the new heaven and earth where the saints will live with Him eternally. God will not allow man's self-destructive bent to interfere with or sabotage His eternal plan of salvation for those who believe.

The Bible, as well as secular history, record some of these "interventions" throughout history. For example:

- God promising salvation to Adam and Eve and denying them access to the tree of life as protection (Genesis 3:24).

- Seth renewing man's worship to God after Cain killed Abel (Genesis 4:26).

- God preserving eight people through the world-wide flood that killed all living humans (Genesis 6:8).

- God choosing Abraham to begin the nation through which He would send the Savior (Genesis 12:1-12).

- God preserving the first century church through Roman persecution (Book of Revelation).

- The city of Jerusalem and Jewish nation destroyed in 70 AD liberating Christianity from Jewish persecution.

- The Protestant Reformation providing the Bible to the masses thus ending Catholic domination (1500-1700s).

- The Restoration movement returning the church's focus to the New Testament for its life and practice (1850s+).

We also see this cycle at work in modern times as well. The theological fall came with the rejection of Bible inspiration and authority in many mainline denominations during the last 75 years. This onslaught was spearheaded by scholars of the "higher critical" method who rejected the inspiration of the Bible seeing it simply as a historical and literary document (historical/literary criticism). These in turn influenced writers, ministers and church leaders to reject Bible authority and rely more on social/psychological/historical sources for teaching about ministry, church life and moral issues (e.g. some Lutheran churches now ordain active homosexuals as ministers because they no longer consider the Bible as an inspired authority on this issue).

The philosophical fall began when nineteenth and twentieth century philosophers established "relativism" as the new basis for thinking about ourselves and our world. Relativism has many variations but basically it says that there are no absolute truths in ethics and that what is morally right or wrong varies from person to person. In other words, the only rules that one is bound by are those one creates for himself or agrees with. In this system of thought the ability to choose trumps God's commands, and social laws become valid when they have been chosen by the majority since they have no value in themselves. Government and law are very important in a relative world because these are the tools used to establish what a society should be.

As a result of the philosophical fall we are currently experiencing the moral fall of the West. This is evident as we see homosexual groups promote their lifestyle to children in schools, government representatives openly use their positions to benefit themselves at the cost of the people they serve, and God's name publicly blasphemed before millions in the media day after day without outrage in response or efforts to stop it. We are witnessing the moral fall of our society when the nation whose motto is "One Nation Under God" now pours adulation on liars, thieves, fornicators, and God haters embodied by many of our popular entertainers and athletes who publicly act this way without shame. When this type of systemic immorality materializes, two possible scenarios are near:

1. Complete moral failure leads to destruction (as it has in the past - flood, Sodom and Gomorrah). However, this time the destruction of the material world will be complete and will signal the return of Jesus and the end of the world (II Peter 3:10).

2. We are near another one of God's "interventions." This would be seen in the working of the Holy Spirit strengthening the church to grow along with a renewed fervor for holy living and service to Jesus by His disciples. This would not simply be a revival of religion in general (not greater Islam, etc.) but the dynamic rise of the church that belongs to Christ.

This cycle of devolution continues throughout history even to this day and it seems that Paul was aware of this historical phenomena as he delineated man's historical fall from grace in the book of Romans.

SUMMARY

Beginning in chapter 1 of Romans, Paul describes how man has fallen from grace and how all humans are caught up in this cycle in one way or another. In chapters 2 and 3 he goes from a macrocosmic (big picture) historical view of this cycle to a microcosmic (detailed) view of the same thing. From the moral history of mankind to the workings of sin in the heart of each individual man, and the results of this not only in the history of nations, but also in the lives of individual people, Jews and Gentiles alike.

The lesson for us is that this cycle continues, and each of us is caught up in it despite our advanced technology and global world view. In the end, there remains only one name under heaven by which we can be saved, Jesus Christ, and the "power of the gospel" is as powerful today as it was when Paul penned these words over 2000 years ago.

When we study the book of Romans we are handling the power that can lead us to a state of grace or ignite a period of grace for the whole world! Such is the power of the gospel that Paul speaks of in Romans 1:16.

3.
Renouncing of Grace
Part 2

ROMANS 2:1-3:12

So far in our study I have said that God's original expression of grace was the creation itself and man's position at the head of it, his participation in the divine nature and intimate contact with God.

The initial fall from grace came when man disobeyed God and in doing so, undermined his position at the head of creation and rendered himself unable to know God intimately.

In chapter 1 of his epistle, Paul describes the process of this fall from a macrocosmic view throughout history:

- **Theological fall** - Man refuses to acknowledge God and refuses to give thanks to God.

- **Philosophical fall** - Man worships something other than God.

- **Moral fall** - Man plunges deeply into active evil.

In response to this we noted that God's renewed expressions of grace (interventions) throughout history always centered around the promise of Christ to come. From the garden to the cross it was the hope of His first coming that prophets continually stirred the people with. From the cross until the end of the world it is the promise of His return that the church revives men's hearts with when sinfulness threatens to overwhelm the moral order.

In the first chapter of Romans, Paul talked about man's moral failure and the things that this led him to. In chapters 2 and 3 he will describe God's judgment and how it will be rendered to all men.

GOD'S METHOD OF JUDGMENT - CHAPTER 2

In chapter 2 Paul summarizes the outworking of God's law which basically decrees that He will judge every single person that ever lived. For the purpose of judgment, the world is divided into two parts: the Jews (all the legitimate descendants of Abraham), and the Gentiles/Greeks (everyone else, not just those from Greece).

God's judgment is described in verses 5-16.

> 5 But because of your stubbornness and unrepentant heart you are storing up wrath for yourself in the day of wrath and revelation of the righteous judgment of God, 6 who will render to each person according to his deeds: 7 to those who by perseverance in doing good seek for glory and honor and immortality, eternal life;

Everyone who pursues good according to God's standard of what is good (the law is what determines this), and does so in the understanding that they seek life with God (honor, glory, immortality), will have eternal life/be saved. Note that this is not a life according to what we think is good, but one lived according to what God thinks is good and doing this consciously. Both Jews and Gentiles who succeed at this will be saved.

> 8 but to those who are selfishly ambitious and do not obey the truth, but obey unrighteousness, wrath and indignation.

Those who do not obey the truth (remember, God is the one who determines truth), who follow their own way, they will be subject to God's exercise of angry punishment.

> [9] There will be tribulation and distress for every soul of man who does evil, of the Jew first and also of the Greek, [10] but glory and honor and peace to everyone who does good, to the Jew first and also to the Greek. [11] For there is no partiality with God.

God will judge every man according to this principle. Those who seek and obey His truth will be blessed and those who do not will be cursed. All will be judged alike, both Jews and Gentiles.

> [12] For all who have sinned without the Law will also perish without the Law, and all who have sinned under the Law will be judged by the Law; [13] for it is not the hearers of the Law who are just before God, but the doers of the Law will be justified.

Gentiles who have not received the Law of Moses are still responsible to the "principle of law" which exists in their conscience and in nature which clearly reveals God's presence and demands. This principle does not articulate and reveal God as clearly as the Jewish Law does, but it does place moral and ethical demands on man nonetheless. For example, even without the revealed Law we know intuitively that killing our parents is not right.

Jews are clearly under the Law of Moses and will be judged according to this Law, which does not contradict the principle of law but merely amplifies it.

Paul explains that the judgment is based not on the sophistication and clarity of the rule we have (principle of law or revealed law), but rather how we respond to what we have.

> [14] For when Gentiles who do not have the Law do instinctively the things of the Law, these, not having the Law, are a law to themselves, [15] in that they show the work of the Law written in their hearts, their conscience bearing witness and their thoughts alternately accusing or else defending them, [16] on the

> day when, according to my gospel, God will judge the secrets of men through Christ Jesus.

Here Paul explains how and why Gentiles are subject to both salvation and condemnation by demonstrating that what saves them or condemns them is their response to the principle of law (directed through conscience and nature) under which they live. He says that when they obey their law, they are righteous just as when the Jews obey the Mosaic Law they are righteous.

> 17 But if you bear the name "Jew" and rely upon the Law and
> boast in God, 18 and know His will and approve the things that
> are essential, being instructed out of the Law, 19 and are
> confident that you yourself are a guide to the blind, a light to
> those who are in darkness, 20 a corrector of the foolish, a
> teacher of the immature, having in the Law the embodiment of
> knowledge and of the truth, 21 you, therefore, who teach
> another, do you not teach yourself? You who preach that one
> shall not steal, do you steal? 22 You who say that one should
> not commit adultery, do you commit adultery? You who abhor
> idols, do you rob temples? 23 You who boast in the Law,
> through your breaking the Law, do you dishonor God? 24 For
> "the name of God is blasphemed among the Gentiles because
> of you," just as it is written.
>
> 25 For indeed circumcision is of value if you practice the Law;
> but if you are a transgressor of the Law, your circumcision has
> become uncircumcision. 26 So if the uncircumcised man keeps
> the requirements of the Law, will not his uncircumcision be
> regarded as circumcision? 27 And he who is physically
> uncircumcised, if he keeps the Law, will he not judge you who
> though having the letter of the Law and circumcision are a
> transgressor of the Law? 28 For he is not a Jew who is one
> outwardly, nor is circumcision that which is outward in the
> flesh. 29 But he is a Jew who is one inwardly; and circumcision
> is that which is of the heart, by the Spirit, not by the letter; and
> his praise is not from men, but from God.

In the final verses he explains that the things that make a person pleasing to God are not the externals of a religion or the level of religious sophistication that one aspires to (Jewish Law revealed God more exactly than the mere principle of law) but how one responded to the law under which he lived.

In chapter 3 Paul describes how well the Jews and the Gentiles have responded to the systems of law they were subject to.

UNIVERSAL CONDEMNATION - CHAPTER 3:1-8

Paul begins chapter 3 by explaining that although the Jews had a true advantage because of the greater clarity of God's will in the Law of Moses (and it was meant to be an advantage), the Jews did not respond to it with righteousness. Their advantage only produced a demonstration of God's goodness, nothing more.

Some were saying (historically recorded) that if God was glorified by the revelation of the Law and His dealing with disobedient Jews, then why did He condemn them? After all, He was being glorified (got what he wanted) was He not? Paul responds that this kind of thinking says that evil glorifies God somehow and for this reason can be justified. The Apostle tells those who are warped enough to think this way that they deserve condemnation because they accuse God of using evil means to obtain a righteous end.

In verses 9-18 he summarizes the universal condemnation due to all men; one that was spoken of in the Old Testament and renewed in the New by Paul.

> 9 What then? Are we better than they? Not at all; for we have already charged that both Jews and Greeks are all under sin;

Both groups have failed to live up to the principle of law under which they lived and so are condemned. Condemned, not because they, the Gentiles, did not become Jews or did not know about Christ, but because of the sins they committed. God does not condemn us because of what we do not know or do not do, but rather for what we actually do.

> 10 as it is written
> "There is none righteous, not even one;
> 11 There is none who understands, There is none who seeks for God;
> 12 All have turned aside, together they have become useless;
> There is none who does good, There is not even one."

The Holy Spirit, using the words of David (Psalm 14:1-3) penned centuries before, declares that God, knowing every heart, judges that none seek Him, none who desire honor, goodness and eternal life. No matter what the outside looks like, God tells us that He sees the condition of the heart.

According to this passage no one is excused or saved through ignorance, why? Everyone can know God through the witness of conscience and nature (Romans 1:19). The one who claims ignorance is simply a person who did not respond to the principle of law under which he lived (Romans 2:23). God assures us that He has examined every heart and none were seeking for Him (Romans 3:10-12). We do not have to judge, God has already done so and recorded the results for us to see.

But someone might say, "What if someone did? What then?"

> And without faith it is impossible to please Him, for he who comes to God must believe that He is and that He is a rewarder of those who seek Him.
> - Hebrew 11:6

Those who respond to God in conscience, nature or law will be found by Him. From Seth to the Patriarchs to the Nation of Israel and now the church, God has always had His people as a light to draw to Him those who searched for Him. In any age or any place, if someone looks for God, God will find them. He is not blind or weak.

SUMMARY

All men have renounced grace and are caught in a cycle of theological, philosophical and moral failure from generation to generation. All, from Adam until the end of the world, are condemned. There is no one that escapes condemnation because of:

Ignorance

All have knowledge of God through the principle of law inherent in nature and conscience, or through direct revelation (the Law of Moses, or today through the Bible and the church).

Innocence

God has and does examine every heart and reveals to us in advance that no one searches for Him and for this reason no one is innocent of sin.

The conclusion is that all have renounced God's initial expression of grace and stand condemned for it. Unless we understand and accept the universality of condemnation:

1. We cannot appreciate God's response of grace in sending Jesus. If condemnation is only partial (even one exception), then Jesus is only a partial Savior and Christianity one of many possible solutions. This is why Christianity is losing its power today, it is not proclaimed as the answer, the only answer.

2. When we accept the universality of condemnation, the great commission (Matthew 28:18-20) takes on more urgency. We have to go because people will perish without the gospel and they will not try to find it themselves. The universality of sin is the reason why evangelism should be the number one priority of the church.

3. The universality of condemnation is a sobering thought that helps us appreciate our own salvation and those who have brought us to Christ as well as those who labor to keep us there.

> I appreciate what I have when I see how close I was to condemnation.

In the next few chapters Paul will explain God's response to universal condemnation, a renewed expression of grace through Jesus Christ.

4.
Response of Grace
Part 1

ROMANS 3:21-25A

In the first chapters of his letter to the Romans Paul has explained that:

1. God initially expressed His grace to man by creating the world and placing human beings at the head of it.

2. Mankind, beginning with Adam, rejected this grace by disobeying God's commands.

3. This disobedience sent him rushing headlong into a cycle of theological, philosophical and moral failure that would ultimately cause mankind to self-destruct if it were not for God's intervention from time to time throughout history.

4. Paul writes that even though man is lost and unable to rescue himself, God has devised a plan that will not only save him from the ongoing cycle of sinful devolution in this life, but also from the punishment he will incur at the judgment to come.

In the last part of chapter 3 the Apostle introduces the next section of his letter which I refer to in this study as, "God's Response of Grace." Here Paul will describe how God answers sinful man's rejection of His initial offer of grace with yet a second offer of grace. In the first instance the Lord created the world and put man at the head of His creation. In the second offer of grace He re-creates man in order to put him into a spiritual kingdom, the church.

What is interesting here is that both of these offers of grace center on mankind and are made possible by Christ. In Colossians 1:16 Paul says that the world was created by and for Christ. In Romans Paul is going to explain that the re-creation of mankind will also be made possible by Christ.

> For by Him all things were created, both in the heavens and on earth, visible and invisible, whether thrones or dominions or rulers or authorities—all things have been created through Him and for Him.
> - Colossians 1:16

The image of Christ as first and last is completed in I Thessalonians 4:13-18 and II Peter 3:10-13.

> 13 But we do not want you to be uninformed, brethren, about those who are asleep, so that you will not grieve as do the rest who have no hope. 14 For if we believe that Jesus died and rose again, even so God will bring with Him those who have fallen asleep in Jesus. 15 For this we say to you by the word of the Lord, that we who are alive and remain until the coming of the Lord, will not precede those who have fallen asleep. 16 For the Lord Himself will descend from heaven with a shout, with the voice of the archangel and with the trumpet of God, and the dead in Christ will rise first 17 Then we who are alive and remain will be caught up together with them in the clouds to meet the Lord in the air, and so we shall always be with the Lord. 18 Therefore comfort one another with these words.
>
> 10 But the day of the Lord will come like a thief, in which the heavens will pass away with a roar and the elements will be destroyed with intense heat, and the earth and its works will be burned up. 11 Since all these things are to be destroyed in this way, what sort of people ought you to be in holy conduct

> and godliness, [12] looking for and hastening the coming of the day of God, because of which the heavens will be destroyed by burning, and the elements will melt with intense heat! [13] But according to His promise we are looking for new heavens and a new earth, in which righteousness dwells.

In these verses the writers explain that at the end of the world it will again be Jesus Christ who will transform the saved from dead bodies to glorious ones, and replace the present physical universe with a completely spiritual kingdom for them to dwell in forever. The grace of God, therefore, was working: a) through Christ to transform us from nothingness to life at the beginning; b) from lost to saved during the cycle of destruction; c) from dead to eternal life at the end of the world.

THE RESULTS OF SIN

Before we examine what Paul says about God's renewed offer of grace, I want to look at the effect that sin has on the individual. We have seen the overview (historical cycle) of mankind falling from grace. I now want us to see how sin affects our relationship with God at close range. I suppose the question to ask in this regard is, "Why is sin so destructive in our lives?" I'd like to mention two reasons:

1. Sin destroys our intimacy with God

Intimacy with God is the substance of spiritual and eternal life. It is what this experience is about.

> This is eternal life, that they may know You, the only true God, and Jesus Christ whom You have sent.
> - John 17:3

A broken fellowship/relationship with God does not simply mean that we are no longer welcome at church. It means that our ability to "see" and perceive the other side, the spiritual dimension, the other reality, the kingdom etc., is severely disabled or destroyed. Sinfulness blurs our vision and our sensitivity to the reality of spiritual things. This is why every sin is dangerous, because each contributes to the lowering of our spiritual vision.

Every bad habit we excuse in ourselves is like a growing cataract that limits our ability to perceive God clearly. Unrepented sins bring us to the point where we can only see this world and not realize that we can no longer see or appreciate the spiritual world. When this happens the preacher becomes a meddler and we resent others who try to point out our weakness and lack of spirituality. Much like elderly folks who sometimes get cranky if we suggest that they get better reading glasses or use hearing aids, everyone else is aware of the problem except them.

2. Sin deprives us of true freedom

> For when you were slaves of sin, you were free in regard to righteousness.
> - Romans 6:20

Living in ignorance of sin frees us from having to deal with the demands of God's laws or our own conscience (not the consequences resulting from disobeying either of these however). But living in sin, ignorant of Christ or in rejection of Christ does not mean that we live in absolute freedom. Freedom from Christ because of ignorance or rejection of Him usually means that we live in slavery to whatever passion or fear that is strongest within us.

This type of slavery works in the same way for the movie star who lives for fame, the homemaker who lives for the next re-modeling project, or the person who lives for the next moment that his or her addiction will be satisfied (caffeine, nicotine, illicit drugs, pornography etc.). We are all slaves. The only question to answer is to whom or what are we enslaved? We cannot always tell from outward appearances because most people create a front in order to hide their sins, but all of us struggle with our allegiances regardless of our gender, social position or intelligence.

Those who are not totally aligned or "enslaved" to Christ are subject to enslavement to something or someone else. The Bible says that at the end there will no longer be any secrets because all secrets will be revealed.

> But if you will not do so, behold, you have sinned against the Lord, and be sure your sin will find you out.
> - Numbers 32:23

MAN'S REACTION WHEN CONFRONTED WITH SIN

Another point I'd like to make concerning sin's effect is how people without faith in Christ deal with sin. Here are a few common tactics:

Denial

When confronted with sin, some people claim that this (whatever this is) is not really a sin or that there is no such thing as sin. Relativism (i.e. What is right or wrong/sinful depends on your point of view) is the most common method used to dispose of any negative feelings created by sin.

Rationalization

Even though people might not be able to describe the process of rationalization, the words they use to defend or justify their behavior clearly reveals this tactic in dealing with sin: "Everybody else does it. I am not so bad. I am not a bad person. This is not such a big deal. A loving God would not condemn me. It's (fill in the blank with favorite minor vice) my only pleasure. Just this once. One last time."

> Human nature moves towards self-justification.
> **- Dietrich Bonhoeffer**

...and I add that ....rationalization is the vehicle that carries the justifier there.

Procrastination

The procrastinator says, "I will deal with this problem/sin when: I am older, stronger, wiser, tomorrow, after the new year, after the retreat, etc."

Procrastination gives this person the feeling that he has actually done something because he has made a decision (to do it later), but the decision never impacts his life because that is the only thing he does, makes a decision.

Delusion

Delusion leads people to think that they are already perfect. These are individuals who think that their sins are so small that God does not even consider them. They believe that since they never committed adultery or murder or the other mortal sins, they are ok. These are usually the ones who are blind to their own selfishness, gluttony, greed, lack of ethics or compassion. The "invisible" kind of sins which are still able to damn them to hell like those of adultery or murder, but are somehow easy to hide from themselves or others. They are selective in their obedience and judgment of themselves and this delusion allows them to create a false image of moral superiority and spiritual maturity when in reality they are among the walking dead already condemned.

Selling Out / Giving Up / Diving In

Another tactic in dealing with personal sin is acknowledging that it exists but not caring. These are the ones who fully enjoy the pleasures and short term advantages of evil in this world with no regard for tomorrow. The greatest danger that they pose is the influence they have on others who admire their worldly confidence and open rejection of God, seemingly without consequences because their lives are often long, successful and satisfying. These are the ones David the psalmist spoke of when he wrote, "The fool has said in his heart, 'there is no God'." (Psalm 14:1).

These are some of the ways that people without faith deal with the very real presence of sin in their lives. For the Christian, however, these attitudes and tactics should be signals that one is losing his spiritual vision.

As I have already stated, sin works to lessen our spiritual vision to the point where we no longer perceive the things of God and instead become attached to the things of this world which have no power to transfer us to the spiritual dimension. In response to this spiritual blindness God sends Jesus, a historical and spiritual lightning bolt who gives sight to everyone who is willing to see and thus, be saved.

RIGHTEOUSNESS BY FAITH
ROMANS 3:21-25A

The text in Romans 3:21-25 explains what God, motivated by grace, has done through Christ to solve the problem of universal sin and its consequences. It reveals how a condemned sinner can be transformed into a saint and live an eternal life in an intimate relationship with God. These four verses hold the core idea of the gospel and the solution to mankind's losing struggle with sin and death.

> 21 But now apart from the Law the righteousness of God has
> been manifested, being witnessed by the Law and the
> Prophets, 22 even the righteousness of God through faith in
> Jesus Christ for all those who believe; for there is no
> distinction; 23 for all have sinned and fall short of the glory of
> God, 24 being justified as a gift by His grace through the
> redemption which is in Christ Jesus; 25 whom God displayed
> publicly as a propitiation in His blood through faith. This was
> to demonstrate His righteousness, because in the forbearance
> of God He passed over the sins previously committed;

These verses become clearer if we understand some of the key words before we try to draw out the meaning of the whole passage:

Law (verse 21)

The revelation to Moses by God, the official title of the Old Testament (including the prophets, ten commandments, etc.) It also refers to the "principle of law" or the idea of a "standard" by which something can be judged.

Righteousness (verse 21)

The quality or state of being just, sound, without prejudice or guilt of any kind.

Faith (verse 22)

This word usually means the belief and trust that something is true, or someone is legitimate. In certain contexts it can also refer to a body of religious teaching (the faith). In this verse it means to believe as true.

Glory (verse 23)

Praise or acknowledgement.

Justified (verse 24)

The means or method by which one becomes righteous. The way one achieves this status. A person is considered innocent, saved or just. One can be justified because one is proven to actually be innocent and thus just or righteous, or one can be justified because the sins one commits are forgiven him.

Grace (verse 24)

A gift or an attitude of benevolence, compassion and generosity. The gift/grace that God gives us is embodied in His merciful attitude towards sinners and their sins.

Redemption (verse 24)

To purchase back, to free, to liberate or to redeem.

Propitiation (verse 25)

This word refers to an appeasement or a peace offering. For example, a man brings flowers home as a peace offering to smooth over a conflict with his wife that he has caused in some way. The flowers are a propitiation. They acknowledge his guilt, his regret and his request for peace between them. Note, however, that in the Bible, it is never man that decides what offering or appeasement is needed in order to be reconciled with God. This is the thinking used in the sacrificial systems for pagan religions (i.e. The people choose something precious that they possess, sometimes their own children, and offer it up to the gods in order to appease their anger or gain their favor). In the Bible it is always God who decides and provides the peace offering / appeasement / propitiation in order to reconcile man back to Himself (e.g. It is as if the wife purchased the flowers and gave them to the husband so that he could offer them back to her in order to smooth over the conflict that he was guilty of creating).

In the Old Testament this word referred to the "mercy seat" or cover that was placed over the ark of the covenant in the Holy of Holies part of the temple. This was the inner chamber where only the high priest was allowed to enter once per year in order to offer sacrifice. The ark was placed in this room. It contained the stone tablets upon which the Ten Commandments were written. Each year, on the Day of Atonement, the high priest would enter and, according to God's command, would sprinkle the blood of a sacrificed animal over the mercy seat as a way of covering and thus cleansing the sins of the people. The priests, who represented the people, would lay their hands on the sacrificial animal symbolically transferring the sins of the people to the animal. The animal would then be killed and its blood offered as a way of removing the sins of the people thus cleansing their consciences of guilt. God's word taught that "life was in the blood" (Genesis 9:4), so through this sacrifice the animal's life/blood was offered to God (by sprinkling it on the mercy seat) as an appeasement/propitiation/peace offering. The idea behind this ceremony was that the mercy seat covered the tablets of the Law which was used to judge and condemn the people for their sins. The blood/life sprinkled over that mercy seat represented the peace offering required to fulfill the demands of the Law for sins committed by the people.

When Paul mentions the word "propitiation" to his readers it summarizes the entire process of offering up a sacrifice, the role of the mercy seat and the idea of a peace offering as a method of dealing with sin before God. It also establishes the basis for understanding the ultimate fulfillment of this ancient Jewish rite. Jesus is the true and final sacrifice, and His blood covers/satisfies the demands of God's Law for restitution/justice/payment due for the sins of all mankind throughout all of history, from Adam's disobedience to the last person standing at the end of time.

This passage, then, explains God's plan and its completion through Jesus Christ, who is the propitiation provided by God to reconcile all mankind back to Himself in peace, never to be separated again by sin.

5.
Response of Grace
Part 2

ROMANS 3:21-31

In the previous chapter, we looked at Paul's summary of man's spiritual situation before God:

- Man, by rejecting God's original offer of grace, finds himself condemned and helpless to change. In other words, man knows what God wants (a sinless life) but is unable to give this to God even if he wants or tries to with all of his might.

This dilemma ushers in God's second offer of grace, which is to save mankind from condemnation and spiritual death through Jesus Christ. Paul explains this second offer of grace in Romans 3:21-25.

TEXT — ROMANS 3:21-25A

> 21 But now apart from the Law the righteousness of God has been manifested, being witnessed by the Law and the Prophets

In previous verses Paul has shown the different ways that God's righteousness (rightness) has been revealed in the past: creation/conscience/the Word or the Law. These, in various ways, demonstrate how good God is and how sinful man is. Now, Paul says, God's righteousness is manifested in yet another way which is not dependent on the Law, but a manifestation that was pointed to or signaled by the Law. In other words the Law, which was necessary to reveal and condemn sin and thus demonstrate how righteous God is in comparison to man, is not necessary to demonstrate God's righteousness in this instance.

> 22a even the righteousness of God through faith in Jesus Christ for all those who believe;

Even (means yes or yea) the righteousness of God that is manifested when a sinful man becomes righteous because of faith/belief in Jesus Christ. God's righteousness is on display when an unrighteous sinner is transformed into a righteous saint through the power of faith without reference to or help from "works" of the Law (human effort). The fact that this transformation is possible and offered to all shows how righteous God really is.

> 22b for there is no distinction; 23 for all have sinned and fall short of the glory of God,

Paul reaches back to previous conclusions made about man's true condition: that he is guilty, helpless and lost. "Falling short of glory" means that man (mankind) is unworthy of God's praise, and Paul has already listed the reasons why this is so:

1. All are guilty of sin.
2. No one is searching for Him.
3. All efforts to reach Him are based on "works of law" strategies.

   Human efforts to please and appease Him are all doomed to failure because they lack purity and timelessness (the two elements that indicate spirituality and divinity). What God's justice requires (a perfect/eternal gift), man can never supply because he is doomed to die (not eternal) and he is impure (imperfect). A perfect and eternal offering is required because this is the result of salvation; man becomes "perfect" again in

God's eyes and he will be equipped to live "eternally" with God in heaven. The offering necessary to purchase this state for sinful man must therefore be equal in value to the intended result.

> [24] being justified as a gift by His grace through the redemption which is in Christ Jesus; [25a] whom God displayed publicly as a propitiation in His blood through faith.

Paul explains why this transformation/re-creation was accomplished and how. Man is declared justified (innocent and therefore righteous) as a gift from God. This status, which is undeserved and unattainable for man, is offered to him by God as a gift because of His compassionate, loving attitude (grace). This is the why. Paul then explains the how. This gift is made possible because Jesus Christ satisfies the justice of God by becoming the appeasement (propitiation) that fulfills the requirements of God's justice which demands punishment for those guilty of sin. God satisfied the demands of His justice publicly by the historical nature of Jesus' death on a Roman cross.

If you were a Jew reading Paul's letter you would understand that God now uses Jesus as the "mercy seat" which was the object upon which the spiritual transaction of atonement was made, formerly located in the Holy of Holies, a dedicated room in the Temple at Jerusalem. Now, this spiritual transaction of atonement is made at a new location: the cross where Jesus was crucified. In addition to this new location, it is Jesus's precious blood that is offered as the appeasement/propitiation for the sins of all men and not the blood of an animal sprinkled on the mercy seat as was the former custom.

If you were a Gentile, you would understand that God pays off man's moral debt by providing Jesus, His only Son, as the payment for sin since we are bankrupt morally and cannot offer to God what is necessary for our own salvation: a perfect and eternal life. God appeases Himself by allowing His Son to suffer and die instead of ourselves.

This gift, Paul says, is received on the basis of faith, it cannot be earned. To see this more clearly in the text it is helpful to place a comma after the word "grace" in verse 24 and after the word "blood" in verse 25.

That man is transformed/re-created from being a helpless, guilty and condemned sinner to a righteous, eternal saint as a gift from God, received on the basis of faith, this shows how righteous God is. Fallen man cannot appease God or move Him with any quality or quantity of human effort. However, man can believe. It is within his emotional, intellectual and spiritual capacity to do so, therefore, God has made this the universal basis for all who seek salvation through Christ.

The proper response to God's free offer of forgiveness is to believe because it is the only thing that all humans can do in an acceptable manner before Him. That God has worked out this plan, accomplished it through Christ, and made it available and attainable to all men through the gospel, this reveals how righteous God truly is. This is God's response to man's rejection of His initial offer of grace, He offers all men the possibility of salvation based on a system of faith, not works. This demonstrates not only His grace towards sinful men but also His personal righteousness.

TEXT — ROMANS 3:25B-31

In verses 25b-26 Paul summarizes the whole affair by declaring that this plan, this method to save man, this second offer of grace does two things.

> 25b This was to demonstrate His righteousness, because in the forbearance of God He passed over the sins previously committed; 26 for the demonstration, I say, of His righteousness at the present time, so that He would be just and the justifier of the one who has faith in Jesus.

1. **It demonstrates God's true righteousness.** God shows how wonderful He is by offering not just one offer of grace but two

offers of grace. The second offer results in the "passing over" of sins previously committed for those who believe. (This doesn't mean that God ignores the sins committed, it means that He forgives the sins committed by those who believe. Unbelievers' sins, however, remain unforgiven.)

2. **God is totally responsible for our salvation.** He is just and requires payment for sins, so in this way He upholds justice. He is also "justifier" (offers mercy), meaning that He works out the way that His justice will be satisfied.

The result is threefold: a) The Law is fulfilled and served; b) Man is saved; c) God is shown to be righteous through it all.

After presenting his case for the Christian faith, Paul goes on to answer questions that would naturally arise from this argument. One such question would be, "What about the Law?" In other words, does a person not accomplish innocence by obeying the Law? Many Jews thought that they were declared innocent by virtue of the fact that they had adequately obeyed the Law of Moses. The best example of this was the attitude of the rich young ruler who came to Jesus asking about eternal life and how to obtain this gift:

> 17 As He was setting out on a journey, a man ran up to Him and knelt before Him, and asked Him, "Good Teacher, what shall I do to inherit eternal life?" 18 And Jesus said to him, "Why do you call Me good? No one is good except God alone. 19 You know the commandments, 'Do not murder, Do not commit adultery, Do not steal, Do not bear false witness, Do not defraud, Honor your father and mother.'" 20 And he said to Him, "Teacher, I have kept all these things from my youth up." 21 Looking at him, Jesus felt a love for him and said to him, "One thing you lack: go and sell all you possess and give to the poor, and you will have treasure in heaven; and come, follow Me." 22 But at these words he was saddened, and he went away grieving, for he was one who owned much property. 23 And Jesus, looking around, said to His disciples, "How hard it will be for those who are wealthy to enter the kingdom of

> God!"
> [24] The disciples were amazed at His words. But Jesus answered again and said to them, "Children, how hard it is to enter the kingdom of God! [25] It is easier for a camel to go through the eye of a needle than for a rich man to enter the kingdom of God." [26] They were even more astonished and said to Him, "Then who can be saved?" [27] Looking at them, Jesus said, "With people it is impossible, but not with God; for all things are possible with God."
> - Mark 10:17-27

This young Jew believed that he had complied with the demands of the Law and yet was somehow dissatisfied with himself. In calling the young ruler to give away his riches to the poor and follow Him, Jesus brushed aside this person's reliance on his superficial compliance to God's commands. What Jesus asked of him reflected the true meaning of the Law which He had previously summarized in Matthew 22:36-40 by saying that to "*love God with all your heart, soul and strength and your neighbor as yourself*" was the greatest of the commandments, and what God (in the person of Jesus) was actually asking this man to do in order to find the answer to his question. Sadly, the young ruler recognized the true demand of the Law in his case but not the identity of the One making that demand. He received the answer to his question, but in doing so discovered that he was unwilling to do what was required and walked away from the One who could give him what he sought after.

In verses 27-31 Paul responds to the question about the possibility of obtaining innocence by complying to the Law by saying that they were mistaken about this point. He reiterates that a person cannot achieve innocence/righteousness through a system of compliance with rules (Law). Righteousness can only be achieved through the system of faith which he outlined before. From now on when he talks about faith and saved by faith, he is including the whole idea of God's grace and offer of forgiveness based on believing in the Savior.

> [27] Where then is boasting? It is excluded. By what kind of law? Of works? No, but by a law of faith.

Paul asks another potential question, "What has eliminated the element of pride concerning man's salvation?" He answers by saying that man's pride is eliminated because he cannot earn his own salvation. Paul argues that each person must receive it based on faith. This system eliminates the possibility of anyone taking credit for their own salvation because no one can do or offer to God anything more than someone else. All can believe, however, and the same thing is thus required of everyone.

> 28 For we maintain that a man is justified by faith apart from works of the Law.

Here, Paul summarizes and confirms his position. He also emphasizes that compliance to rules merits nothing insofar as gaining innocence is concerned because compliance to rules never gives you back the purity that sin causes you to lose. This purity is given back to you as a person saved by faith, and once you have it you can then have a relationship with God once again. This is the essence of salvation. It is not an object that you obtain through personal effort, it is an experience you are permitted to have because of what God, through Christ, has done for you.

> 29 Or is God the God of Jews only? Is He not the God of Gentiles also? Yes, of Gentiles also, 30 since indeed God who will justify the circumcised by faith and the uncircumcised through faith is one.

The system of salvation by faith is universal in that both Jews and Gentiles are saved in the same way and by the same God.

Another question: "Do we abolish the Law (Law of Moses/Principle of Law) if we accept salvation by faith?"

> 31 Do we then nullify the Law through faith? May it never be! On the contrary, we establish the Law.

The true nature and purpose of the Law is fully explained and established when we understand the principle of salvation on the basis of faith. Paul clarifies this in chapters 5:20 and 7:7-25. Basically, the purpose of the Law is to reveal sin and pronounce judgment upon it. He teaches that there is a sequence to this:

1. The Law reveals how and to what extent we fall short.

- The Mosaic Law did this in a historical context for the Jews.
- The Principle of Law did this in a philosophical context. (We do not do what we ought to do. We know this through observation, reasoning and the urging of our conscience.)

2. Once the Law reveals sin, it then reveals to the sinner the consequences of sin: guilt, shame, dread of death and eternal suffering.

3. At this point man has several options in his reaction to the Law's accusation and condemnation of personal sin:

    1. Ignore it and face the consequences.
    2. Embrace sinfulness fully despite the knowledge and warning of the Law. This leads to the cycle of falling Paul talked about earlier.
    3. Try to obey the Law and thus avoid judgment and punishment. If someone attempts to do this, several things may occur.

        a. They may become hypocrites thinking they have succeeded. (Those who are as comfortable in the pew as they are in the world. The Pharisees were a good example of this type of hypocrisy.)

        b. They may become slaves to the Law, always trying to live up to its demands. Religious people who are active in their religiosity without joy. These are usually against any move towards compassion and grace because these mean freedom, and they do not want anyone to be free while they themselves are slaving away at perfect law-keeping. The older brother in the parable of the Prodigal Son is one of these.

c. Some become discouraged and fall into spiritual depression when faced by the unbending demands of the Law. In the modern day these are the ones who go from church to church looking for the right answer, or the perfect situation, and usually end up quitting and angry at the church instead. Judas was this type of person.

d. Those who cry out for mercy, who realize that they are helpless before the demands and judgment of the Law. These say to God in all honesty, "I am not able to do what you want; I want to but I am not able; I need your mercy; I need your grace or else I am lost." The person who is at this point will finally meet Jesus and understand what salvation by "faith" really means.

Paul explains that the Law brings you to the threshold of grace, but faith in Christ is what brings you into the state of grace.

6.
Response of Grace
Part 3

ROMANS 4

Let us review once again the details surrounding God's response of grace. God's initial expression of grace was the creation itself and the placing of man at the head of it. Man, by his disobedience of God's command, rejected this gift and, as a result, experienced a headlong fall from grace that was and continues to be manifested in a cycle of spiritual and moral degeneration. Paul explains in Romans that God responded to this rejection of grace by man with a second offer of grace which he outlines in Romans 3:21-6:23.

In these verses he explains that with this second offer of grace:

1. God pays man's moral debt through the death of Jesus (Romans 3:21-25a).
2. God offers guilty man forgiveness and regeneration based on faith in Jesus (Romans 3:25b-26).
3. God proclaims that salvation is accomplished through a system based on faith in an individual and not one of compliance to a standard (Romans 3:21-26).

Once Paul shows how and why God saves us, he then answers questions that might arise as a result of this teaching. For example, questions involving the role of the Law: "If we are saved on the basis of faith in an individual and not compliance to the rules, what purpose does the Law have, or has it been abolished altogether?" Paul replies that the Law's role is to reveal sin (Romans 3:20) and, as such, will always be necessary in service to the gospel. The gospel does not remove the Law, it reveals its proper purpose and legitimacy (Romans 3:31).

> Do we then nullify the Law through faith? May it never be! On the contrary, we establish the Law.
> - Romans 3:31

The next question would naturally come from the Jews. They would ask, "Well, what about Abraham? Did not his compliance to God's will establish his righteousness, and is not this state of salvation reserved only for Jews anyways?" The next section of Paul's epistle deals with this subject.

ABRAHAM AND RIGHTEOUSNESS

ROMANS 4:1-25

> 1 What then shall we say that Abraham, our forefather
> according to the flesh, has found? 2 For if Abraham was
> justified by works, he has something to boast about, but not
> before God. 3 For what does the Scripture say? "Abraham
> believed God, and it was credited to him as righteousness."

Paul states here that Abraham's righteousness (innocence / acceptability) before God was based on faith. This is what Abraham learned through his experience with God (remember the definition of faith we are working with: believing as true what God has said despite indications to the contrary and acting upon that belief).

> 4 Now to the one who works, his wage is not credited as a
> favor, but as what is due. 5 But to the one who does not work,
> but believes in Him who justifies the ungodly, his faith is
> credited as righteousness, 6 just as David also speaks of the

> blessing on the man to whom God credits righteousness apart from works:
> 7 "Blessed are those whose lawless deeds have been forgiven,
> And whose sins have been covered.
> 8 "Blessed is the man whose sin the Lord will not take into account."

Paul argues that for the one who earns righteousness by compliance to rules, his innocence is not bestowed as a gift but is his wage based on his success at compliance. He is not saying that it is possible to actually do this, only that if it were possible, God would owe it to that person to judge him as innocent, this would only be fair. However, for the person who is declared innocent because he believes God's promise, this is a favor from God not a wage, a favor given because of faith. Paul then refers to a familiar figure and story in Jewish history to make his point.

He quotes the psalmist David, as David echoes the words of a grateful man who has been forgiven on account of faith. In his affair with Bathsheba (II Samuel 11:1-12:25), David was guilty of adultery, premeditated murder in having her husband, Uriah, killed in order to take her as his own wife, and deception in lying to the nation concerning these despicable actions. According to the Law, David should have been removed as king and executed.

However, Nathan, the prophet sent by God to confront David about his sins, said, "You are forgiven" after the repentant king acknowledged his wrongdoing (II Samuel 12:1-14). Because he believed the words of the prophet, David was forgiven and allowed to carry on with his life, fully righteous again before God. To be sure, David paid a heavy price for his sins (the child he and Bathsheba conceived died, and there would be continued strife in his family until he himself died), but David was renewed as a righteous man before God. His soul was safe from destruction despite his terrible sins because he chose to believe that God forgave him, and not because he made restitution of some kind for the adultery, murder and lies that he committed (the restitution/payment for his moral debt was paid by Jesus on the cross).

> [9] Is this blessing then on the circumcised, or on the uncircumcised also? For we say, "Faith was credited to Abraham as righteousness."

Now Paul deals with the question, "To whom was this blessing meant for? To Abraham and all his descendants only or to all men?" The Jews read the Word and thought that it was only for Abraham's descendants.

> [10] How then was it credited? While he was circumcised, or uncircumcised? Not while circumcised, but while uncircumcised;

Paul answers this with a question, "When was righteousness offered, when Abraham was circumcised or not?" The answer, of course, is that he was considered righteous at a time when he had not yet been circumcised. The sign (circumcision) that bound all Jews together was given after God declared that Abraham was righteous because of his faith. The unmistakable conclusion from a Jewish perspective was that righteousness by faith was originally offered to a Gentile.

> [11] and he received the sign of circumcision, a seal of the righteousness of the faith which he had while uncircumcised, so that he might be the father of all who believe without being circumcised, that righteousness might be credited to them,
> [12] and the father of circumcision to those who not only are of the circumcision, but who also follow in the steps of the faith of our father Abraham which he had while uncircumcised.

Here, Paul gives a reason for this. Abraham was declared righteous through faith while uncircumcised so that all Gentiles thereafter might identify with him as uncircumcised people who, like Abraham, responded with faith, in order to become righteous. These are his spiritual descendants because they, like Abraham, became righteous through faith.

In the same way, his biological descendants (the Jewish people) became his spiritual descendants, not by being circumcised (this was the sign that they were part of God's chosen people), but by emulating his faith. His true descendants were not those tied to him biologically (Jewish culture) or religiously (circumcision), but those who were made righteous by faith as he was (the advantage of being culturally and religiously related to Abraham was that the revelation concerning righteousness through faith would be revealed to them first through Jesus before it would be revealed to the Gentiles).

> 13 For the promise to Abraham or to his descendants that he would be heir of the world was not through the Law, but through the righteousness of faith. 14 For if those who are of the Law are heirs, faith is made void and the promise is nullified; 15 for the Law brings about wrath, but where there is no law, there also is no violation. 16 For this reason it is by faith, in order that it may be in accordance with grace, so that the promise will be guaranteed to all the descendants, not only to those who are of the Law, but also to those who are of the faith of Abraham, who is the father of us all, 17 (as it is written, "A father of many nations have I made you") in the presence of Him whom he believed, even God, who gives life to the dead and calls into being that which does not exist.

Paul reiterates that salvation is obtained for everyone through a system of faith, and all who try to secure it by compliance to rules will fail. Salvation is a promise made to those who believe, and trying to earn it through compliance changes it from a promise to a salary.

"Where there is no law, there is no violation." This means that when one is obtaining salvation without reference to the Law (as one does when obtaining it though faith), that person does not violate the Law by doing so. In other words, the Gentiles who believe do not desecrate the Law by doing so. This system of salvation by faith makes it fair for everyone, Jew and Gentile alike.

> 18 In hope against hope he believed, so that he might become a father of many nations according to that which had been spoken, "So shall your descendants be." 19 Without becoming

> weak in faith he contemplated his own body, now as good as dead since he was about a hundred years old, and the deadness of Sarah's womb; [20] yet, with respect to the promise of God, he did not waver in unbelief but grew strong in faith, giving glory to God, [21] and being fully assured that what God had promised, He was able also to perform. [22] Therefore it was also credited to him as righteousness.

In this passage Paul reviews the history and context of Abraham's faith. Remember, faith is believing God's Word/promise as true, despite the evidence to the contrary, and acting upon it.

God never gave Abraham a Law, rituals, specific rules of conduct or a moral code. God made him a promise that he would be blessed with a son and that eventually his descendants would grow into a great nation and have their own land. God asked Abraham to believe that He would do this for him. Paul says that Abraham believed God's promise would be fulfilled despite the evidence to the contrary (e.g. Abraham was a nomad in a foreign land and did not own any property; he and his wife grew old and beyond child bearing age without having a natural son). Abraham continued to believe that God would accomplish these things for him, and because he continued to believe despite the evidence to the contrary, God declared him to be innocent/righteous (despite his many failures).

> [23] Now not for his sake only was it written that it was credited to him, [24] but for our sake also, to whom it will be credited, as those who believe in Him who raised Jesus our Lord from the dead, [25] He who was delivered over because of our transgressions, and was raised because of our justification.

Paul now brings the matter into the present tense. Abraham is a model for faith, the type of faith that believes God and His promises as well as the reward that these promises bring. Today, Paul says the substance of what we are to believe is different than what Abraham was called on to believe. God's promises to us are not of children or land or descendants. His promises are for forgiveness, bodily resurrection from the dead and eternal life. However, the nature of our response to His promises is the same as it was for Abraham. We are called upon to believe that Jesus' death pays for our sins; believe that God forgives us, declares us righteous and innocent, and will resurrect us from the dead when Jesus returns. Believing God, and believing that what He promises will actually be given to us, this is what makes us righteous.

SUMMARY — TAKE THE FAITH TEST

ANSWER YES OR NO

1. Do you believe that Jesus is the Son of God and, after dying on a Roman cross and being buried for three days, resurrected from the dead? Do you believe this even though you did not see any of it with your own eyes?

2. Do you believe that Jesus, by His sacrifice on the cross, makes restitution to God for all of your sins?

3. Do you believe that you are innocent, righteous, acceptable and ready to go to heaven right this moment if God called you now?

4. Do you believe that, despite the wrinkles, arthritis, soreness, disease and sure death that you face, God will resurrect you one day to be consciously with Him forever in heaven?

5. Have you acted upon your belief by expressing your faith in repentance, baptism (immersion in water) and faithfulness to Him?

If you have answered yes to these five questions, I am happy to say that you have the faith of Abraham and are one of his true spiritual descendants. Your **faith** has made you righteous in God's eyes just as Abraham's faith did this for him.

7.
Response of Grace
Part 4

ROMANS 5

After setting forth the basis of the gospel message (that man is considered worthy of eternal life based on his faith in Jesus and not in how perfectly he obeys the Law), Paul now goes on to respond to four questions his readers may have based on what he has just taught.

Question #1:

What about the Law, does the gospel message void the Law?

Answer:

Salvation by faith demonstrates the nature and purpose of the Law, which is to reveal sinfulness and the condemnation that results from it. This revelation should bring man to search for mercy and forgiveness which is ultimately found in the gospel. As far as the gospel is concerned, this is the purpose of the Law, not its only purpose but its ultimate purpose.

Question #2:

What about Abraham, how did he become righteous without the Law?

Answer:

Abraham was considered righteous because he continued to believe that God would fulfill His promise to him, even when it seemed hopeless. Abraham was not righteous because he was perfectly obedient, he was righteous because he continued to believe God despite his failures. Those whose faith is like Abraham's are righteous even if their lives are imperfect.

In this chapter, we will look at a third possible question that Paul's teaching might produce among his readers.

WHAT SALVATION DOES FOR ME?

ROMANS 5:1-21

Until this point Paul has talked about why salvation was necessary (universality of sin), how it was accomplished (atonement of Christ), and upon what basis was it received (faith in Jesus Christ).

Question #3:

What does this salvation do for me?

A Jewish reader might say, "After all, before Christ we had the Law, the prophets, the temple and we were God's chosen people. What advantage does salvation in Christ bring us?" In the same way a Gentile could say, "Before Christ we were free to do whatever we wanted, we were a law unto ourselves. How does salvation through Christ benefit us?"

Answer:

Paul answers both groups by enumerating six blessings that come with salvation by grace through faith in Jesus Christ.

1. Peace with God

> [1] Therefore, having been justified by faith, we have peace with God through our Lord Jesus Christ, [2a] through whom also we have obtained our introduction by faith into this grace in which we stand;

Salvation produces a clear conscience and freedom from fear, guilt and shame. A saved person can talk to God openly with knowledge that He hears and is sympathetic to his prayers, something that was difficult for Jews and impossible for Gentiles.

2. Joy

> [2b] and we exult in hope of the glory of God. [3] And not only this, but we also exult in our tribulations, knowing that tribulation brings about perseverance; [4] and perseverance, proven character; and proven character, hope;

Salvation in Christ produces a joy based on the hope that Christians will ultimately triumph over suffering and death. The trials of everyday life serve to strengthen a Christian's character, not destroy it. This is because trials, for Christians, are always viewed from an eternal perspective, not a temporal one. What seems hopeless for the unbeliever is only a temporary reversal for the one with a promise of eternal life.

Perseverance (proven experience) creates hope as believers see over and over again how God sustains them in different ways through various difficulties. This builds confidence (hope) that this pattern of God's help will continue (and this confidence shows in their character). However, this hopeful view of life is only possible for the faithful believer in Jesus.

3. Love

> [5] and hope does not disappoint, because the love of God has been poured out within our hearts through the Holy Spirit who was given to us.

Being saved does not suddenly enable a person to be more loving and kind. This comes with practice and maturity. Being saved, however, leads believers to the realization that God loves them! Those who are justified become conscious of God's love through the indwelling of the Holy Spirit who works in them in a variety of ways. For example:

- A strengthened prayer life (Romans 8:26).
- Comfort during times of trial (Acts 9:31).
    - For unbelievers comfort comes through a sense of stoicism or acceptance/resignation to the inevitable.
    - For Christians it is a conscious comfort and hope in Christ produced by the presence of the Spirit within them.
    - For Jews the Holy Spirit only empowered certain leaders among them (kings/prophets/judges) for a time and a specific purpose. They had a promise that the Holy Spirit would be available to all, but only in the future when the Messiah would come (Joel 2:28-29).
- A motivation to love others and do them good as a result of the promptings of the Spirit within, replacing former attitudes of selfishness and other weaknesses of the sinful flesh.

In these and many other ways Christians experience the love of God working within themselves. Jews had a knowledge of the Holy Spirit but not a personal experience of His power. Gentiles had neither the knowledge nor the experience of Him since they were mired in the superstitious rituals of their pagan religions.

4. Assurance / Security – vs. 6-10

Christ's death pays for all of our sins. In addition to this, His resurrection and continued presence serves to assures us that we will continue to be saved.

> [6] For while we were still helpless, at the right time Christ died for the ungodly. [7] For one will hardly die for a righteous man; though perhaps for the good man someone would dare even to die. [8] But God demonstrates His own love toward us, in that while we were yet sinners, Christ died for us.

We know how much God loved us and wanted us saved because He sent Jesus to die when we were at our very worst, when we hated Him. This knowledge builds confidence in His love for us.

> [9] Much more then, having now been justified by His blood, we shall be saved from the wrath of God through Him. [10] For if while we were enemies we were reconciled to God through the death of His Son, much more, having been reconciled, we shall be saved by His life.

Paul completes the argument by saying that if Jesus was ready to die for us when we hated Him, imagine what He will do for us now that we believe and love Him, and He is alive and able to receive that love?

Christians have great security in the knowledge that their Savior is alive and active in making sure that they remain saved.

5. Reconciliation

> [11] And not only this, but we also exult in God through our Lord Jesus Christ, through whom we have now received the reconciliation.

Different English versions of the Bible use the word "atonement" or "propitiation" here. This was an Old Testament word meaning "to cover," originally referring to the cover over the ark located in the Holy of Holies part of the temple. In time this word evolved to mean the "appeasement" or "payment" for sin.

In this context, it refers to the sacrifice and the reason that it was offered. Paul refers to an exchange or a change (atonement/reconciliation) of a very special nature. It is the change on one party induced or caused by the action of another. In the Bible it is not man who does something to "change" God's attitude towards him. This is the basis of pagan and occult thinking that use all manner of rituals and incantations in order to change or manipulate their gods' and spirits' attitude so that they will show favor to those offering the rituals.

In the Bible, it is God who does something to change man's condition. God changed His relationship with lost man from judge to redeemer, and sent Jesus to eliminate (pay for/redeem) man's sins. This action on God's part changed man from being a guilty, condemned sinner to becoming a righteous saint. This change (reconciliation) is also a constant source of joy (exultation) for both parties. Man will enjoy it for as long as God does, and God will enjoy it forever.

6. Eternal Life - vs. 12-21

The Law revealed sin and its consequences: death. The Jewish sacrificial system was built around the exposition of man's sins and the reminder that death was the punishment due on account of sin (millions of animals were sacrificed over many centuries to highlight these truths). In this passage Paul highlights the two ultimate realities of life and death by going back to Adam since he was the first to live and the channel through which sin, and consequently death, originally entered the world. In order to explain the benefit of eternal life, he must first explain the source of sin and its destructive result: death.

> 12 Therefore, just as through one man sin entered into the
> world, and death through sin, and so death spread to all men,
> because all sinned— 13 for until the Law sin was in the world,
> but sin is not imputed when there is no law. 14 Nevertheless
> death reigned from Adam until Moses, even over those who

> had not sinned in the likeness of the offense of Adam, who is a type of Him who was to come.

Paul reminds his readers that sin entered humanity through Adam, and death entered through sin which ultimately spread to all men because all men eventually sin. Man is not subject to death because he is born guilty of sin but because, like Adam, he has sinned through disobedience.

Here, Paul explains that theoretically, a person cannot be charged with committing an offense if there is no revealed law of some kind that exists. However, he goes on to make two other observations:

1. There was no revealed law during the time between Adam and Moses.

2. People died anyways.

His conclusion is that even though the Law was not revealed to man during this time, its principles were still in operation. This is similar to our experience with the law of gravity. It was explained by Newton in 1678, but even without his discovery and explanation of gravity's principles or laws, people were nevertheless aware of this phenomena, subject to it, and responded to its existence by observation and intuition. In other words, people were subject to the law of gravity long before it was explained scientifically.

In the same way, Paul says that people were subject to God's Law and were affected by it long before it was clearly articulated and recorded by Moses. Adam was an example of this and so were those who, even though they did not sin as grievously as he did, were subject to God's Law and bore the consequences for breaking it (i.e. God's spiritual law said that if one disobeyed God's command they would die).

Paul mentions those who did not sin in the likeness of Adam's sin. Adam's sin was greater than those who sinned after him because:

- He had no cumulative weakness of the flesh.

- He had intimate knowledge of God and yet he sinned.
- He had great privilege and opportunity but sinned anyways.

His great sin brought death to him, and even though subsequent sins by those who came after him were lesser in comparison to Adam's sin, these people still suffered the consequence of death because of their own sins (e.g. Person A is killed by a bomb and person B dies from a single bullet. In the end both are dead). The conclusion is that all sin causes death to the soul of man.

In the same passage Paul also says that Adam, even in his sinfulness, was a "type" or preview of Christ:

Adam

- Original in form
- First of the human race
- Channel for sin and death

Christ

- Only begotten
- First among the resurrected
- Channel for forgiveness and life

In the last few verses of this chapter, Paul will compare the significance of what came through Adam (sin and death) to what came through Moses (Law and condemnation) to what eventually comes through Christ (forgiveness and eternal life).

> 15 But the free gift is not like the transgression. For if by the transgression of the one the many died, much more did the

> grace of God and the gift by the grace of the one Man, Jesus Christ, abound to the many.

The sinfulness that came through Adam was great but the grace that brings forgiveness for those sins is greater, it needs to be in order to cover sins.

> 16 The gift is not like that which came through the one who sinned; for on the one hand the judgment arose from one transgression resulting in condemnation, but on the other hand the free gift arose from many transgressions resulting in justification.

The result of sin is condemnation, but Christ brings innocence. What Christ provides is not only greater in power but also better in quality. Christ brings justification that leads to peace, joy, etc. Sin only brings guilt, fear and death. The "experience" of what Christ brings is superior in quality than what the Law brings.

> 17 For if by the transgression of the one, death reigned through the one, much more those who receive the abundance of grace and of the gift of righteousness will reign in life through the One, Jesus Christ.

Sin brings death, Christ brings supremacy over death which is eternal life.

> 18 So then as through one transgression there resulted condemnation to all men, even so through one act of righteousness there resulted justification of life to all men.
> 19 For as through the one man's disobedience the many were made sinners, even so through the obedience of the One the many will be made righteous.

Here Paul summarizes what he has just said: Adam/sin equals condemnation and death; Christ/atonement equals justification, righteousness and eternal life.

> [20a] The Law came in so that the transgression would increase;

Paul makes a parenthetical statement here. He explains again why the Law was originally given, not to eliminate sin and death but to clearly reveal and condemn it.

> [20b] but where sin increased, grace abounded all the more, [21] so that, as sin reigned in death, even so grace would reign through righteousness to eternal life through Jesus Christ our Lord.

The Law, in revealing sin and death, served as an instrument to also highlight the power of God's grace revealed in the work and person of Christ. This grace is shown to:

1. Be wide and deep enough to cover the ugliest sin in nature or quantity.

2. Powerful enough to change the sentence hanging over man from death to eternal life.

Paul proclaims that mankind is saved by faith and he describes the wonderful blessings that come with this salvation: peace with God, joy with God, love of God, safety with God, reconciliation with God and eternal life with God. He also emphasizes the fact that all of this is "only" available through faith in Jesus Christ

8.
Response of Grace
Part 5

ROMANS 6:1-14

So far in our study of grace based on the book of Romans we have seen that:

1. God originally expressed His grace in creating the world and placing man at the head of it.

2. Man rejected this grace and became trapped in a cycle of sin and death from which he had no power to free himself.

3. God offered a second expression of grace by doing several things:

    a. Paid man's moral debt through the sacrifice of Jesus.

    b. Offered man forgiveness and eternal life based on faith in Christ rather than perfect adherence to the Law.

4. After explaining these things, Paul answers four questions that might arise based on his text thus far:

    a. What about the Law, do we abolish it when we accept salvation by faith? Answer: no, we see its true purpose which is to reveal sin and lead men to ask for mercy.

b. What about Abraham, was he not justified by obedience to God? Answer: no, he was considered righteous because he believed. His obedience was never perfect, but it was motivated by what he believed. Because of that he was counted righteous.

c. What does this system (righteousness based on faith in Christ) accomplish for me, does it give me what I had before? Answer: much more! Previously through the Law, the Jews only had the knowledge of sin and death, and through the prophets a promise of hope in the future. Now, Paul tells them that they have the fulfillment of the promises through Christ (peace with God, joy with God, love from God, reconciliation with God and eternal life with God).

In this section, we will examine the answer to the final question posed.

A NEW ATTITUDE — ROMANS 6:1-23

What is the relationship between sin and grace? Paul poses this question twice (verse 1 and 5) and answers it in two different ways (verses 2-14 and 16-23).

Historical Answer - Romans 6:1-14

> 1 What shall we say then? Are we to continue in sin so that grace may increase?

The subtext of this question is as follows: If grace is always greater than sin, why not continue to sin in order to generate more of God's grace? Why not just relax and enjoy sin, it will produce more grace anyway?

The answer that Paul gives to the Christian who might ask such a question is: something took place in your past that has changed not only the direction of your life but the attitude that you have toward sin. To think that one could take advantage of God's grace (as the question suggests) is the way you used to think about such things, but something happened. You do not think like that anymore. Why?

> [2] May it never be! How shall we who died to sin still live in it? [3] Or do you not know that all of us who have been baptized into Christ Jesus have been baptized into His death?

Paul answers by stating that we, as Christians, cannot purposefully and easily enjoy sinning anymore after dying to sin. Dying to sin actually involves several deaths for the ones who believe in Christ. For example:

- The death of ignorance to the reality of sin. A Christian cannot enjoy sin anymore because he knows the Law.

- The death of enjoyment of sin because now the believer has the knowledge of the gospel (the price paid to redeem sins) and is conscious, through the Spirit, that God is present and aware of him. This is why some people are reluctant to hear the gospel or talk about the Bible, they suspect that it will ruin their appetite for sin.

- The death of the old life (sinful attitudes and habits) through the action of baptism. At baptism God puts Christ between the Christian and his old life. This is why Christians cannot enjoy sin like they used to, Christ is in the way.

> [4] Therefore we have been buried with Him through baptism into death, so that as Christ was raised from the dead through the glory of the Father, so we too might walk in newness of life. [5] For if we have become united with Him in the likeness of His death, certainly we shall also be in the likeness of His resurrection, [6] knowing this, that our old self was crucified with Him, in order that our body of sin might be done away with, so that we would no longer be slaves to sin; [7] for he who has died is freed from sin.

- The death of the rule of sin over believers.
    - Before Christ, we were ruled by our passions and lusts for money, sex, power, enjoyment, control, fame, etc.
    - Paul says that when death to sin occurred in baptism it signaled the death of the rule of sin over us and the beginning of a new life, a new rule, one where sin is not the ruler, but Christ is the ruler.
    - In baptism, the rule of sin is broken by Christ in four ways.
        - We receive forgiveness and this unburdens our consciences (Acts 2:38; I Peter 3:21).
        - We enter into a relationship with God where He considers us with mercy instead of judgment and this relieves our fear. We are now righteous (Galatians 3:26).
        - We receive the presence of the Holy Spirit (Acts 2:38) who enables us to pray and resist the temptation that once overcame us (Romans 8:13); we now have the kind of power where we control the sin in us and not the other way around.
        - We enter into a fellowship with other believers (church) which gives us comfort and courage when we are weak and when we fail (Acts 2:47).
    - Sin cannot rule over a person who has a clean conscience, the forgiveness for sin continually available (I John 1), the ability to resist its drawing power and a relationship with others who also have these blessings. These things are received at baptism.
- The death of "death" itself. If sin no longer rules, then death is defeated because death is the result of sin.

- It is the punishment for those who are found guilty of sin.

- When one is pardoned for sin then the punishment is excused. Here we speak of the death or suffering of the soul for eternity.

> [8] Now if we have died with Christ, we believe that we shall also live with Him, [9] knowing that Christ, having been raised from the dead, is never to die again; death no longer is master over Him.

Our resurrection will resemble Christ's in that it will be to an eternal life where death will no longer be present. We will suffer physical death here on earth because our physical bodies have been weakened by sin. After the resurrection, however, our glorified bodies will have no sin and so death will no longer be possible.

> [10] For the death that He died, He died to sin once for all; but the life that He lives, He lives to God. [11] Even so consider yourselves to be dead to sin, but alive to God in Christ Jesus.

Paul summarizes the matter. The death Christ experienced was in relationship to sin. He took responsibility for our sins, and for this reason death had a claim on Him and thus He experienced it (the Law of sin and death was meted out to Him). Once He did so, however, His experience with death was over. His resurrection no longer related Him to our sins, they were left in the grave along with the death He paid for them. His existence now is in relationship to God in heaven where He has returned to reign (at the right hand of God, Mark 16:19).

In the same way, those who have ended their relationship with sin (in baptism) should leave sin and the desire for it in the grave and be totally focused on God. In other words, Jesus left our sins in the grave, we leave our sins in the water; Jesus rose from the grave, we too have risen from the waters of baptism as new creatures in Christ (II Corinthians 5:17);

and as Jesus ascended into heaven, we also will rise from the dead and ascend to be with Him forever (I Thessalonians 4:17).

The original question was, "Why not continue to sin in order to generate more grace (since grace is always greater than sin)?"

The answer to this question is that we do not sin to provoke grace because our attitude and relationship towards sin has changed since our baptism. Before baptism, sin was master and it led us to all forms of disobedience and impurity. When we were baptized we died to sin, and with this death sin ceased its rule over us, but not its presence in us (Paul will deal with this situation in the next chapter). He will also explain how we can increase the influence of grace in our lives but it will not be by increasing our sin (this type of thinking was the result of a sinful and darkened mind in the first place).

> 12 Therefore do not let sin reign in your mortal body so that you obey its lusts, 13 and do not go on presenting the members of your body to sin as instruments of unrighteousness; but present yourselves to God as those alive from the dead, and your members as instruments of righteousness to God. 14 For sin shall not be master over you, for you are not under law but under grace.

Paul finishes this section by encouraging them to be aggressive in dealing with their sins, but to do so they have to willingly submit to God and His will for their lives in the first place.

9.
Response of Grace
Part 6

ROMANS 6:15-23

After presenting the gospel as God's offer to save man in response to man's faith in Christ, Paul proceeds to answer several questions that may arise from his teaching. One objection was the idea that if God is gracious to us as sinners, what motivation do we have to avoid sin? This objection is expressed in two questions in Romans 6 and answered in two different ways.

In Romans 6:1 the question was: Since God's grace always expands to accommodate greater and greater sin, why not just relax and remain in sin knowing that grace will cover it? Paul responds to this question by explaining that once we come into this grace, we die to sin (in the waters of baptism) and no longer see or participate in sin in the same way that we did before we knew God's grace.

AN EXPERIENTIAL CHANGE
ROMANS 6:15-23

Paul again poses a similar question in verse 15 but responds to it in a different way in verses 16-23.

> 15 What then? Shall we sin because we are not under law but under grace? May it never be!

This time the question about grace is posed in the following manner: Just because our salvation is offered to us based on our belief in Jesus and not on perfect obedience to the Law, does this mean we can disobey the Law (sin) without guilt or fear?

Before, Paul answered this type of question from a "historical" perspective by saying that we do not pursue sin anymore because something happened in our past (at baptism) where sin lost rulership over us and we now have a different view of sin. In verses 16-23 Paul will answer this second question "experientially" by saying that since that historical moment, the grace of God has produced a new experience for us, an experience he will refer to as "eternal life."

In the Bible, the concept of eternal life does not only refer to a period of time (e.g. time without end) but also a quality of spiritual life experienced now and in the future. This new experience of "eternal life" is made up of different elements:

1. The knowledge of our personal righteousness with God. Consciously being aware that we are acceptable to God is part of the "eternal life" experience.

2. The discernment of the change in our character brought about through the inner workings of the Holy Spirit (usually referred to as the process of sanctification). I am aware that I am not the same person I used to be and recognize the person I am becoming in Christ.

3. The lessening of the fear of death and the growing assurance of our resurrection from the dead.

The point Paul will make in answer to the question is: This eternal life experience that I enjoy under grace motivates me to obey and serve God much more than my old experience of the dread of condemnation and punishment under the Law ever did.

> 16 Do you not know that when you present yourselves to
> someone as slaves for obedience, you are slaves of the one

> whom you obey, either of sin resulting in death, or of obedience resulting in righteousness?

Here Paul states the case in general terms: If you serve sin, the experience will be death; if you serve Christ, the experience will be life, eternal life.

> [17] But thanks be to God that though you were slaves of sin, you became obedient from the heart to that form of teaching to which you were committed, [18] and having been freed from sin, you became slaves of righteousness.

Paul now refers back to the historical moment when one believes as true the message of the gospel and responds in faith expressed through repentance and baptism. As Paul explained before, this response effectively frees us from sin in that we die to it at this point. The motivating factor for Christians now is to do what Christ leads us to do (the pursuit of righteous living). We grow in our awareness of this as our understanding of the Bible deepens and our sensitivity to the Holy Spirit within us grows.

> [19] I am speaking in human terms because of the weakness of your flesh. For just as you presented your members as slaves to impurity and to lawlessness, resulting in further lawlessness, so now present your members as slaves to righteousness, resulting in sanctification.

He exhorts them to pursue what is good and right with the same enthusiasm that they pursued sin in the past, knowing that the rewards are much greater.

> [20] For when you were slaves of sin, you were free in regard to righteousness.

He reminds them that when sin ruled over them and they accepted that rule, Christ did not and could not motivate them. This is why we should not be disappointed when people who are not "in Christ" (those who have not had that historical experience) act in ways which are unchristian. Only Christians act like Christians. A person cannot be motivated by Christ without the historical experience with Christ (buried with Christ in baptism, Romans 6:4).

> 21 Therefore what benefit were you then deriving from the things of which you are now ashamed? For the outcome of those things is death.

He also reminds them of the outcome of this rulership of sin: shame and, ultimately, condemnation and death.

> 22 But now having been freed from sin and enslaved to God, you derive your benefit, resulting in sanctification, and the outcome, eternal life.

He compares that experience to the new experiences one has since the historical break with sin: righteousness (I am acceptable to God), sanctification (Christ likeness), and eternal life (the experience of assurance in an eternal future with God).

> 23 For the wages of sin is death, but the free gift of God is eternal life in Christ Jesus our Lord.

Paul summarizes by stating the outcome of both experiences: sin leads to death and Christ leads to life.

Paul's answer to the question, "If God responds to my sin with kindness rather than Law, why should I not continue to enjoy my sin?" is as follows:

Those who experience God's kindness are motivated not to sin. In other words, I pursue righteousness much more strenuously under grace than I ever did while I was under Law. Why? Because under the Law, the harder I tried to obey, the more I realized my imperfections. The more I knew the Law, the greater awareness I had of my sins. Greater knowledge and greater effort to obey the Law only widened the gap between myself and God. It was like looking into a mirror, the longer and closer I looked at my reflection, the more imperfections I began to notice.

Under grace, however, every effort that I make to please God, every new revelation I understand about Christ, every step I take in the process of sanctification leads to a greater awareness of His presence, His wisdom, His power and His love. In Christ (under grace) greater knowledge, greater service and greater spiritual maturity actually close the gap between myself and God, and produce joy, peace and love within me in the process. This is why I pursue righteousness, this effort rewards me with the experience of being close to God, a feeling I have not had before. Pursuing sin brings me further away from God and I do not want that now that I know what being close to God feels like.

Therefore, the answer to the question, "If I am under grace and not Law, why avoid sin?" is this, "I avoid sin as a Christian under grace because pursuing righteousness is more rewarding than pursuing sin."

OUR QUESTION

The Jews asked:

"If we are under grace, should we not be free to sin?"

Answer:

No, you died to sin in baptism and no, pursuing righteousness is more profitable.

Of course, this is not the question that we, in the church today, ask. Our question is different. Our question is, "What is the relationship between grace and the good works that we do?" In other words, "If I am under grace, what good are my good deeds and how many of these are enough?" or, "I am saved with or without good deeds, so why bother?"

This question suggests a lack of understanding concerning the true purpose of good works done by Christians. Our good works are done not to justify ourselves or to earn God's favor or forgiveness, they are done as evidence of our faith.

In answer to the question, "What good are my good works if I am under grace?" The answer is that my good works are useful to God as evidence of my faith in Jesus Christ who has the power to reward my faith, not my works.

My good works:

- Cannot justify me (take my sins away). Only the cross can do this (I Peter 2:24).

- Cannot make me more righteous. Only faith in Christ can accomplish this (Philippians 3:9).

- Cannot endear me to God. Only faith and perseverance in Christ can do this (John 1:12).

Good works are done as a witness to others that I believe in Jesus, and are a method to provoke those who see my good works to glorify and praise God themselves (Matthew 5:16). In another epistle Paul says that our good works have actually been prepared in advance by God for us to do so that others who witness them will glorify and praise Him (Ephesians 2:10).

The relationship between grace and works is that grace motivates me to do good works in order to witness for Christ and provoke others to glorify God (if not now, then when Jesus returns when all works will be revealed). Good works are always seen by God and never wasted.

You can tell the difference between good works motivated by grace and those motivated by other reasons (pride, pragmatism, etc.). Works motivated by grace glorify God, not man. They are Christ centered, biblically supported and powered by the Holy Spirit. Works motivated by grace produce peace of mind, unity among Christians and joy to those they reach. Works motivated by other factors, however, often produce envy, division and discouragement. At best they relieve human suffering and sometimes enlighten, but only for a short time.

In the end, if you have truly understood this series on grace and allow God's grace to touch your hearts, the result will be a greater and freer motivation to do good, not in order to achieve perfection but to evidence a sincere faith, glorify God and provoke others to seek out the same experience. These works prompted by these motives will bless others, edify the one who does the good and honor God.

10.
Saved yet Struggling

ROMANS 7

Paul has explained how God's renewed offer of grace has saved man from sin and the condemnation of the Law, and he also answered several probable questions based on his teaching of saved by grace through faith.

In chapter 7 he will deal with another question and provide his own experience as the answer to that question. In this chapter he asks, "If I am saved and under grace, why do I continually struggle with sin?" In other words, "If I am in the power of grace why am I still tempted by sin?"

Struggling

In chapter 6 Paul explains that in baptism we die with Christ and we are resurrected to a new experience in Christ, and I detailed what that experience was like (eternal life). In chapter 7 he goes on to say that this "new life" is not without its problems and struggles.

There has been a debate about whether Paul is speaking of his former life here or if he is describing his present life as a Christian. There are sincere arguments for both sides, however, I believe that Paul is speaking of his present state for two reasons:

1. The entire section deals with the new life one experiences after being buried with Christ in baptism. Paul is continuing his description of this new life (chapter 6 described the "upside" of this life - freedom from fear and death, and power in the Holy

Spirit etc.; chapter 7 describes the downside). This downside occurs when the duality of man's natures collide (the new man living inside the old sinful flesh).

2. In verse 25 he summarizes the entire chapter in the present tense suggesting that the experience he describes in chapter 7 is one that he is now undergoing.

Chapter 7 could be entitled, "Saved Yet Struggling." Paul tells his readers, "We are truly saved and you can see the result of it in your lives, however, while you are in the flesh you will still struggle with sin." In this chapter Paul describes the struggle in his own life. In the next he will offer the solution that God provides.

The essential problem that Christians face, which Paul explains here, is that in becoming united to Christ and having a new life we are no longer subject to the Law in judgment but we are still influenced by the Law in effect. In other words, the Law no longer condemns us before God, but it still has the power to effect our lives here on earth.

This idea of being free from the Law, Paul explains in chapter 7:1-6.

> 1 Or do you not know, brethren (for I am speaking to those
> who know the law), that the law has jurisdiction over a person
> as long as he lives? 2 For the married woman is bound by law
> to her husband while he is living; but if her husband dies, she
> is released from the law concerning the husband. 3 So then, if
> while her husband is living she is joined to another man, she
> shall be called an adulteress; but if her husband dies, she is
> free from the law, so that she is not an adulteress though she
> is joined to another man.
> 4 Therefore, my brethren, you also were made to die to the
> Law through the body of Christ, so that you might be joined to
> another, to Him who was raised from the dead, in order that
> we might bear fruit for God. 5 For while we were in the flesh,
> the sinful passions, which were aroused by the Law, were at
> work in the members of our body to bear fruit for death. 6 But
> now we have been released from the Law, having died to that

> by which we were bound, so that we serve in newness of the Spirit and not in oldness of the letter.

Paul uses the analogy of marriage to demonstrate that the Law has limits. The Law governed marriage until a partner died, after which the person was beyond the Law (not beyond God). Those in Christ have another power source: grace, not Law.

> [7] What shall we say then? Is the Law sin? May it never be! On the contrary, I would not have come to know sin except through the Law; for I would not have known about coveting if the Law had not said, "You shall not covet." [8] But sin, taking opportunity through the commandment, produced in me coveting of every kind; for apart from the Law sin is dead. [9] I was once alive apart from the Law; but when the commandment came, sin became alive and I died; [10] and this commandment, which was to result in life, proved to result in death for me; [11] for sin, taking an opportunity through the commandment, deceived me and through it killed me. [12] So then, the Law is holy, and the commandment is holy and righteous and good.

In verses 7-12 the Apostle reassures his readers that just because one is beyond the Law does not mean that the Law has failed or the Law is in some way imperfect. On the contrary, the Law has done its job, it has convicted Paul of sin and made him aware that he was condemned. This is the essential purpose of the Law in its relationship to man: to convict and condemn, and ultimately lead one to Christ for forgiveness and salvation. By performing these tasks the Law remains suited for its intended purpose, and thus is perfect, holy and without fault.

In the final section Paul will describe the nature of the struggle that takes place within himself as a saved spirit dwelling inside a sinful flesh that is not judged by the Law anymore, but affected by it.

> [13] Therefore did that which is good become a cause of death for me? May it never be! Rather it was sin, in order that it

> might be shown to be sin by effecting my death through that which is good, so that through the commandment sin would become utterly sinful.

First of all, Paul asks another rhetorical question, "How can something good and holy (the Law) cause death?" Paul answers that it is sin that causes death, the Law merely exposes sin by holding it up to the light of perfection, and condemns it by revealing God's response to sin. The Law does not cause the suffering and death experienced by the flesh, it is a diagnostic tool God uses to show us that it is sin that actually causes human misery. For example, an x-ray does not cause or cure cancer, it reveals the cancer that a person suffers from. When the disease is revealed, anguish and suffering are heightened.

> 14 For we know that the Law is spiritual, but I am of flesh, sold into bondage to sin. 15 For what I am doing, I do not understand; for I am not practicing what I would like to do, but I am doing the very thing I hate. 16 But if I do the very thing I do not want to do, I agree with the Law, confessing that the Law is good. 17 So now, no longer am I the one doing it, but sin which dwells in me.

Paul explains this struggle from a personal perspective and notes several things about it:

1. The essential reason for the struggle is that a regenerated spirit dwells in the sinful shell of flesh.

2. The regenerated spirit recognizes and desires to practice the Law (previously codified in the Law of Moses for the Jews, now embodied in the words of Christ - Matthew 28:20), but the sinful flesh undermines any attempt to do so. What makes the struggle so painful is that a Christian is aware of this dichotomy at all times.

When he says that he is no longer the one doing it, Paul does not reject personal responsibility for his sins because of his struggle. He means that when he sins, he has failed to do what he really wants to do, obey

God's Law. Sin is a victory of his flesh, not his spirit. It is, he admits, still his flesh however.

> 18 For I know that nothing good dwells in me, that is, in my flesh; for the willing is present in me, but the doing of the good is not. 19 For the good that I want, I do not do, but I practice the very evil that I do not want. 20 But if I am doing the very thing I do not want, I am no longer the one doing it, but sin which dwells in me.
> 21 I find then the principle that evil is present in me, the one who wants to do good. 22 For I joyfully concur with the law of God in the inner man, 23 but I see a different law in the members of my body, waging war against the law of my mind and making me a prisoner of the law of sin which is in my members.

In these verses Paul describes the outcome of this struggle between the regenerated spirit and the flesh. He sees clearly the desire of his regenerated spirit to do God's perfect and holy will, as well as his sinful flesh's unwillingness to respond. The struggle brings to light the opposite forces in his nature. He also sees clearly which of the two has the preeminent position. It is his "inner man," his "spirit," his "regenerated self," that wills, that recognizes, that delights, that desires to do God's will. The flesh is a power, a force, a resister that frustrates these desires, but it is not the dominant force in his life.

He concedes that this struggle will continue throughout his lifetime (a prisoner) and he must accept the situation.

The final verses summarize what he has explained in the previous section.

> 24 Wretched man that I am! Who will set me free from the body of this death?

This situation (to be continually denied the desire of his inner man by the influence of his sinful flesh) is wretched. The body of death he refers to is his sinful flesh that will not allow a complete union and harmony between his regenerated spirit and God. This ongoing struggle moves him to cry out to God for help, "Who will set me free?"

Paul answers his own question in the next verse.

> 25 Thanks be to God through Jesus Christ our Lord! So then, on the one hand I myself with my mind am serving the law of God, but on the other, with my flesh the law of sin.

The solution is twofold:

1. Jesus Christ: Paul does not explain all that Christ does to help us, he simply says that the solution is in Christ. In chapter 8 he will describe how God helps us deal with this particular struggle.

2. Acceptance: The struggle is painful and frustrating, but is easier to bear once accepted for what it is.

Paul explains that as a regenerated man, he serves God honestly and sincerely with His spirit, and when he sins the flesh is responsible. This is not to absolve him of responsibility, but rather to confirm the existence of both entities and which one influences his obedience or disobedience.

SUMMARY

This is every Christian's struggle. Do not think that Paul was unique or that his struggle was more intense than the average Christian of today. What he describes is the normal struggle that each one of us experiences as we try our best to serve Christ and see how short we fall at times. This is not an excuse for lukewarmness, but it does help us to understand why even knowing and wanting to do our best for Christ does not always guarantee the results we desire. The flesh also has its say.

The struggle is really a sign of life. Do not be discouraged if what you see in Christ is not always what you accomplish in Christ. The fact that you see, the fact that you desire, the fact that you hurt is the proof that Christ is in you and that you are truly a regenerated person. The unregenerated man, whether he is an unbeliever or a Christian in name only, is always easy to spot: he has no struggle.

Although he only mentions it briefly in chapter 7, Paul knew that God would and did provide for his struggle. He provides help and encouragement in this life so that we do not lose hope or desire for the next life. He provides a promise of eternal life so that we know that one day the struggle will end.

11.
The Request of Grace

ROMANS 8

In the previous chapter, we looked at the final section in Paul's epistle that dealt with God's response of grace to man's sins. In chapter 7 he explains that even though grace saves us through faith, there is a constant struggle in our lives because the new regenerated man must dwell in the confines of sinful flesh. Grace saves the soul but does not eliminate the suffering and struggle caused by sin in the body, and this experience is felt by every Christian.

In chapter 8 the Apostle describes the demands of this grace and how God enables us to meet these demands.

Grace demands and empowers at the same time. It demands that we live spiritual lives no longer slaves of sin, and it provides us the two things that enable us to do this.

1. Grace Provides Justification

> Therefore there is now no condemnation for those who are in Christ Jesus.
> - Romans 8:1

This verse is the high point of the section we have just finished and the summary statement for all that has been said so far. That we are not condemned by God for what we are guilty of doing is called, being justified.

In today's language "justified" usually means that we have a good cause or good reason to do something. It suggests that we have a good excuse for what we have done. In biblical usage it means that we have been found innocent, or that we are considered not guilty (even if we have committed the crime).

The first seven chapters of the book of Romans explained how God accomplished this "justification" on our behalf through Jesus Christ, and why. To summarize: we were guilty of sin and were condemned to hell because of it. Nothing we could say or do could change the judgment upon us. Because of His grace, God sent Jesus to suffer the punishment of death for us, and because of His sacrifice, our sins were paid for. God then offered this innocence (justification) to those who believed and obeyed the gospel.

This is how grace provides justification for sinners. This is why there is now no condemnation for those who are in Christ Jesus, because those who are in Christ (associated/linked/with Jesus through baptism) have been justified. There is now no condemnation if you are justified.

However, God's grace demands that you live a "spiritual" life and now that you are justified, you can do so. Why?

- There are no sins that separate you from God. He now looks favorably upon you. Your prayers, your actions and your efforts to please Him are acceptable because you are acceptable.

- You know what spiritual living is. Christ who justifies you also reveals, in His Word, what spiritual living is all about (a lifestyle very different from your old one).

- You have hope. There is no motivation to live spiritually if there is no hope of heaven. Jesus guarantees our acceptability to God and our entrance into heaven through His death and resurrection.

The first way, therefore, that grace provides for the spiritual lifestyle that it demands is by assuring us that we are innocent before God and will be with Him one day in heaven, despite the struggle with sin we continue to experience here on earth.

2. Grace Provides for Sanctification - Romans 8:2-39

Justification is a one time event. You are never any more innocent, acceptable or justified as the day you come out of the waters of baptism. You cannot become more innocent, sin free, acceptable or righteous in the eyes of God than on the day you are justified by the blood of Christ as you confess His name in the waters of baptism. For example, a newborn baby is as alive as a 50 year old man. The baby cannot become any more "alive" physically than on the day of its birth. In the same way, the day you are justified is the day you are "born again," the day you become alive in Christ. Nothing you do can make you more alive or more saved than you were on that day.

However, a baby can develop, mature and grow in its skills and appreciation of life. In the same way, a Christian can (and must) develop, mature and grow in his skill to appreciate and function in the spiritual world. If the baby does not grow, it will remain helpless and die. If the Christian does not grow, he will also die spiritually.

This process of spiritual maturation and growth is called sanctification. Justification is a one time even that makes us alive or born again in Christ. Sanctification is a lifetime process of growth and development that ends when the physical body is shed in death, and the fully formed spiritual body emerges to be with God in heaven eternally.

Grace provides for this sanctification process by giving us the Holy Spirit. In the book of Acts, Peter explains how one obtains justification ("...repent and be baptized in the name of Jesus for the forgiveness of your sins" - Acts 2:38a). He then mentions that those who are justified in this way receive the gift of the Holy Spirit ("...and you shall receive the gift of the Holy Spirit" - Acts 2:38b). He does not mention why we receive Him, or what the Holy Spirit will do within us. It is left to Paul in the eighth chapter of Romans to explain that the Holy Spirit is given to dwell within each Christian in order to complete the process of sanctification in that person. Jesus, therefore, accomplished justification by dying on the cross for us, and the Holy Spirit accomplishes sanctification by dwelling within us.

In verses 2-29 Paul explains how the Holy Spirit works to accomplish this sanctification within every believer.

1. The Spirit Leads Us

> 2 For the law of the Spirit of life in Christ Jesus has set you free
> from the law of sin and of death. 3 For what the Law could not
> do, weak as it was through the flesh, God did: sending His own
> Son in the likeness of sinful flesh and as an offering for sin, He
> condemned sin in the flesh, 4 so that the requirement of the
> Law might be fulfilled in us, who do not walk according to the
> flesh but according to the Spirit. 5 For those who are according
> to the flesh set their minds on the things of the flesh, but those
> who are according to the Spirit, the things of the Spirit. 6 For
> the mind set on the flesh is death, but the mind set on the
> Spirit is life and peace, 7 because the mind set on the flesh is
> hostile toward God; for it does not subject itself to the law of
> God, for it is not even able to do so, 8 and those who are in the
> flesh cannot please God.
> 9 However, you are not in the flesh but in the Spirit, if indeed
> the Spirit of God dwells in you. But if anyone does not have the
> Spirit of Christ, he does not belong to Him. 10 If Christ is in you,
> though the body is dead because of sin, yet the spirit is alive
> because of righteousness.

The Holy Spirit provides the Word of God (II Peter 1:20-21), gifts to serve (Romans 12:1; I Corinthians 12:1-11) and encouragement to do what is right (I Thessalonians 5:19). In all of these ways He directs the way that a spiritual person should go. Living according to the Holy Spirit's direction contributes to our spiritual maturity.

2. The Spirit Resurrects Us

> [11] But if the Spirit of Him who raised Jesus from the dead dwells in you, He who raised Christ Jesus from the dead will also give life to your mortal bodies through His Spirit who dwells in you.

The final step in the process will occur after death and it is the Holy Spirit that will resurrect the believer from the grave. Sanctification is only a taste and a glimpse of what is to come, and the Holy Spirit guarantees that He has the power to resurrect us by demonstrating this power in resurrecting Christ before us.

3. The Spirit Empowers

> [12] So then, brethren, we are under obligation, not to the flesh, to live according to the flesh— [13] for if you are living according to the flesh, you must die; but if by the Spirit you are putting to death the deeds of the body, you will live. [14] For all who are being led by the Spirit of God, these are sons of God.

Sin is what causes separation from God, and through the power of the Holy Spirit we are able to gain the upper hand over sin in our lives. This is important because we want to keep a close relationship with God and enjoy the fellowship with Him that produces our peace, joy and assurance. The more we overcome sin, the closer God draws near to us. The Holy Spirit is critical in helping us overcome the sin in our lives.

4. The Spirit Comforts

> [15] For you have not received a spirit of slavery leading to fear again, but you have received a spirit of adoption as sons by which we cry out, "Abba! Father!" [16] The Spirit Himself testifies with our spirit that we are children of God, [17] and if children, heirs also, heirs of God and fellow heirs with Christ, if indeed we suffer with Him so that we may also be glorified

> with Him.
> 18 For I consider that the sufferings of this present time are
> not worthy to be compared with the glory that is to be
> revealed to us. 19 For the anxious longing of the creation waits
> eagerly for the revealing of the sons of God. 20 For the creation
> was subjected to futility, not willingly, but because of Him
> who subjected it, in hope 21 that the creation itself also will be
> set free from its slavery to corruption into the freedom of the
> glory of the children of God. 22 For we know that the whole
> creation groans and suffers the pains of childbirth together
> until now. 23 And not only this, but also we ourselves, having
> the first fruits of the Spirit, even we ourselves groan within
> ourselves, waiting eagerly for our adoption as sons, the
> redemption of our body. 24 For in hope we have been saved,
> but hope that is seen is not hope; for who hopes for what he
> already sees? 25 But if we hope for what we do not see, with
> perseverance we wait eagerly for it.

We have been justified, promised heaven and told that God loves us, but as we look around we see ourselves weak and sinful. In addition to this difficult reality we observe that everything around us, including ourselves, is dying. We also witness the terrible injustice and violence that exists unabated in the world. The Holy Spirit works to sustain our hope in salvation despite the evidence we see to the contrary. He helps us to continue believing and hoping in the face of relentless attacks by Satan and the mocking of an unbelieving world.

5. The Spirit Prays for Us

> 26 In the same way the Spirit also helps our weakness; for we
> do not know how to pray as we should, but the Spirit Himself
> intercedes for us with groanings too deep for words; 27 and He
> who searches the hearts knows what the mind of the Spirit is,
> because He intercedes for the saints according to the will of
> God.

The Holy Spirit is God and, as God, He knows our hearts and the mind of God as well. He guarantees that our prayers come before the Deity in an acceptable way, always wrapped in faith toward Christ. We are physical, sinful and limited to the material world. The Holy Spirit makes our communication with a spiritual Being possible and profitable for us.

6. The Spirit Protects Us

> 28 And we know that God causes all things to work together
> for good to those who love God, to those who are called
> according to His purpose. 29 For those whom He foreknew, He
> also predestined to become conformed to the image of His
> Son, so that He would be the firstborn among many
> brethren; 30 and these whom He predestined, He also called;
> and these whom He called, He also justified; and these whom
> He justified, He also glorified.
> 31 What then shall we say to these things? If God is for us, who
> is against us? 32 He who did not spare His own Son, but
> delivered Him over for us all, how will He not also with Him
> freely give us all things? 33 Who will bring a charge against
> God's elect? God is the one who justifies; 34 who is the one who
> condemns? Christ Jesus is He who died, yes, rather who was
> raised, who is at the right hand of God, who also intercedes for
> us. 35 Who will separate us from the love of Christ? Will
> tribulation, or distress, or persecution, or famine, or
> nakedness, or peril, or sword? 36 Just as it is written, "For Your
> sake we are being put to death all day long; We were
> considered as sheep to be slaughtered."
> 37 But in all these things we overwhelmingly conquer through
> Him who loved us. 38 For I am convinced that neither death,
> nor life, nor angels, nor principalities, nor things present, nor
> things to come, nor powers, 39 nor height, nor depth, nor any
> other created thing, will be able to separate us from the love
> of God, which is in Christ Jesus our Lord.

Once we are justified, the Holy Spirit's work is to make sure that the evil one does not destroy our souls. He works all things for the good of our salvation. We can deny the Holy Spirit and willingly permit Satan to come into our lives, and in so doing lose our salvation. However, without that invitation and our willing cooperation to abandon Christ, Satan can no longer capture or possess us. The Holy Spirit works to guarantee our growth and development in Christ, as well as our protection from Satan and his schemes.

In these verses, Paul describes the various ways that the Holy Spirit enables our growth and development in Christ, a process called sanctification:

- He directs us in how we should live.
- He empowers us to overcome sin.
- He comforts our fears, doubts and pain.
- He helps our prayer life.
- He protects us from the evil one.
- He resurrects us from death.

SUMMARY

God's grace demands that we live spiritual lives (and we want to do this because grace ignites this desire within us). Spiritual living, however, requires two important things. Thankfully, God's grace also provides the things we need to live that spiritual life: complete justification through Christ and complete sanctification through the Holy Spirit.

In the following chapters (9-11) Paul will write about those who refused grace and why they did so, and then he will finish his epistle (chapters 12-16) by describing what living by grace looks like in everyday life.

12.
The Refusal of Grace

ROMANS 9-11

In chapters 7-8 Paul answers questions on how God provides for saved people, even though they are sinners. In chapters 9-11 he responds to yet another question, but this time one dealing less with the gospel itself and more with the Jewish nation. Two key doctrines among Evangelicals come from this passage and so we will discuss it in light of these at the proper time.

The question that Paul answers in this section of his epistle is, "Why were the Jews not saved?" This question would be coming from the Gentiles rather than the Jews themselves.

Chapter 9

> 1 I am telling the truth in Christ, I am not lying, my conscience
> testifies with me in the Holy Spirit, 2 that I have great sorrow
> and unceasing grief in my heart. 3 For I could wish that I
> myself were accursed, separated from Christ for the sake of
> my brethren, my kinsmen according to the flesh, 4 who are
> Israelites, to whom belongs the adoption as sons, and the
> glory and the covenants and the giving of the Law and the
> temple service and the promises, 5 whose are the fathers, and
> from whom is the Christ according to the flesh, who is over all,
> God blessed forever. Amen.
> 6 But it is not as though the word of God has failed. For they
> are not all Israel who are descended from Israel; 7 nor are they
> all children because they are Abraham's descendants, but:

> "through Isaac your descendants will be named." [8] That is, it is not the children of the flesh who are children of God, but the children of the promise are regarded as descendants.

Paul frames the question in the following way, "If the Jews had all the advantages, why did they fail to obtain salvation? Did the Law fail them?" The Apostle then answers these questions by arguing that the Law (Word) did not fail. It brought salvation to whom salvation had been promised. The promise, however, was not based on culture and heredity but on God's Word. (Verses 6-8 establishes the basic premise for the entire argument.)

Paul gives several examples where he shows that God's Word is the basis for determining what happens, not man's will, his works nor his culture.

> [9] For this is the word of promise: "At this time I will come, and Sarah shall have a son." [10] And not only this, but there was Rebekah also, when she had conceived twins by one man, our father Isaac; [11] for though the twins were not yet born and had not done anything good or bad, so that God's purpose according to His choice would stand, not because of works but because of Him who calls, [12] it was said to her, "The older will serve the younger." [13] Just as it is written, "Jacob I loved, but Esau I hated."

Example #1 – Rebekah

She was told by God's Word that her older son would serve her younger son, and despite every human effort to change this, Esau, the older son, ended up serving Jacob, her younger son.

> [14] What shall we say then? There is no injustice with God, is there? May it never be! [15] For He says to Moses, "I will have mercy on whom I have mercy, and I will have compassion on whom I have compassion."
> [16] So then it does not depend on the man who wills or the man

> who runs, but on God who has mercy. [17] For the Scripture says
> to Pharaoh, "For this very purpose I raised you up, to
> demonstrate My power in you, and that My name might be
> proclaimed throughout the whole earth."

Example #2 – Moses

God clarified to the great Jewish leader, by His Word, why this Egyptian king had ascended to such power. So that by his defeat the greatness of God could be revealed to all the world throughout history.

> [19] You will say to me then, "Why does He still find fault? For
> who resists His will?" [20] On the contrary, who are you, O man,
> who answers back to God? The thing molded will not say to
> the molder, "Why did you make me like this," will it? [21] Or
> does not the potter have a right over the clay, to make from
> the same lump one vessel for honorable use and another for
> common use? [22] What if God, although willing to demonstrate
> His wrath and to make His power known, endured with much
> patience vessels of wrath prepared for destruction? [23] And He
> did so to make known the riches of His glory upon vessels of
> mercy, which He prepared beforehand for glory, [24] even us,
> whom He also called, not from among Jews only, but also from
> among Gentiles. [25] As He says also in Hosea,"I will call those
> who were not My people, 'My people,' And her who was not
> beloved, 'beloved.'"
> [26] "And it shall be that in the place where it was said to them,
> 'you are not My people,' There they shall be called sons of the
> living God."
> [27] Isaiah cries out concerning Israel, "Though the number of
> the sons of Israel be like the sand of the sea, it is the remnant
> that will be saved; [28] for the Lord will execute His word on the
> earth, thoroughly and quickly." [29] And just as Isaiah foretold,"
> Unless the Lord of Sabaoth had left to us a posterity, We
> would have become like Sodom, and would have resembled
> Gomorrah."

Example #3 - The Jewish people

By the Word of God, through the prophets, they were told that they would be called to receive God's promise. This example of how God's Word is sure and never fails its intended purpose acts as a bridge towards the final verses in which Paul makes a point about the Jews and why they failed to receive the promise.

God's Word, the Law, did not fail the Jews concerning salvation (he has just shown that the Word never failed anyone concerning anything). It was the Jews who failed the Word and by doing so missed the promise. "Why did this happen?" he then asks.

> [30] What shall we say then? That Gentiles, who did not pursue righteousness, attained righteousness, even the righteousness which is by faith; [31] but Israel, pursuing a law of righteousness, did not arrive at that law. [32] Why? Because they did not pursue it by faith, but as though it were by works. They stumbled over the stumbling stone, [33] just as it is written, "Behold, I lay in Zion a stone of stumbling and a rock of offense, And he who believes in Him will not be disappointed."

1. The Jews tried to obtain righteousness through adherence to rule of law rather than by what the Word of God said which was righteousness through faith. God's Word never fails, if it says by faith, then it is going to be by faith.

2. They rejected Jesus, the Savior, and in so doing lost the promise that He brought (forgiveness and eternal life).

The Word was able to deliver on its promises, but on its conditions, not man's conditions. The Jews failed because they did not accept the Lord in the way that the Word of God required them to do so.

CHAPTER 10

In this next section Paul argues that God has always based the reception of His promises on faith. Some maintain that in the Old Testament God offered His blessings and promises to man based on a system of Law, and in the New Testament He does so based on a system of faith and grace. This is incorrect.

In this section, Paul responds to this issue by quoting Isaiah and other Old Testament prophets who taught that God's blessings and salvation have always been obtained based by faith and never by adherence to a system of law.

> 8 But what does it say? "The word is near you, in your mouth
> and in your heart"—that is, the word of faith which we are
> preaching, 9 that if you confess with your mouth Jesus as Lord,
> and believe in your heart that God raised Him from the dead,
> you will be saved; 10 for with the heart a person believes,
> resulting in righteousness, and with the mouth he confesses,
> resulting in salvation. 11 For the Scripture says, "Whoever
> believes in Him will not be disappointed."

Many (Evangelicals) see these verses as the expression of faith one must make in order to be saved (to say, "I believe"). In other words, they go to these verses in order to find the answer to the question, "How shall I respond to the gospel?" And the answer they find here is to say, "I believe and accept Jesus as my Savior." However, the correct expression of our faith in response to the gospel is described in Romans 6:2-9 (buried with Him in baptism, etc.) where Paul is specifically talking about the gospel and how one expresses their faith in response to it, not Romans 10 where the Apostle is describing how God used the system of Law and the system of faith.

In Romans 10, Paul is quoting Old Testament prophets in order to demonstrate that salvation by a system of faith was always what the Word taught. This was not a new teaching that he was introducing. In the Old Testament, that faith was first expressed by circumcision. If you were not circumcised you were not part of the people of God (i.e. even Moses was threatened with death for not circumcising his son, Exodus 5:24-26). In the New Testament we are also saved by faith, but we express that faith through repentance and baptism (Mark 16:16; Acts 2:38), and not by repeating an oral religious formula.

The point of this passage is that, as it has always been, the Word guarantees that all who call upon God in faith will be saved, and in Romans chapter 6 Paul explains that the proper expression of faith in response to the gospel is repentance and baptism.

> 16 However, they did not all heed the good news; for Isaiah says, "Lord, who has believed our report?" 17 So faith comes from hearing, and hearing by the word of Christ.
> 18 But I say, surely they have never heard, have they? Indeed they have;
> "Their voice has gone out into all the earth,
> And their words to the ends of the world."
> 19 But I say, surely Israel did not know, did they? First Moses says,
> "I will make you jealous by that which is not a nation,
> By a nation without understanding will I anger you."
> 20 And Isaiah is very bold and says, "I was found by those who did not seek Me,
> I became manifest to those who did not ask for Me."
> 21 But as for Israel He says, "All the day long I have stretched out My hands to a disobedient and obstinate people."

Here, Paul makes the point that in the Old Testament the people heard the Word first through the prophets, then they heard it through Christ and His Apostles. This Word always promised salvation by faith, but the people did not respond to it. Even this rejection was known and recorded by God in His Word. Paul says that God's Word did not cause this rejection, but it did predict and record it. This prediction ironically demonstrates how God's Word never fails and serves as one more example of this principle: the Word never fails, even in predicting the infidelity and failure of the Jews themselves to whom God's Word was first revealed and entrusted.

CHAPTER 11

Another question arises. A "but" question, "But the Word says that God will preserve and save His people, Israel. Has God failed in this? Has the Word been incorrect?" Paul answers this line of questioning in chapter 11. He says, "No! Even among the Jews there are some who have received the promise by faith." He is referring to people who would have been familiar to his readers:

- Peter and the 12.
- 500 disciples mentioned in I Corinthians.
- 3000 at Pentecost.
- Jews who believed with Paul's missionary work.

In Romans 1, Paul explained that those who reject God are permitted to disengage from Him.

> And just as they did not see fit to acknowledge God any longer, God gave them over to a depraved mind, to do those things which are not proper
> - Romans 1:28

In the same way the prophets spoke of those among the Jews who would be let go because God does not keep a person or people against their will.

> 7 What then? What Israel is seeking, it has not obtained, but those who were chosen obtained it, and the rest were hardened; 8 just as it is written, "God gave them a spirit of stupor, Eyes to see not and ears to hear not, Down to this very day."
> 9 And David says, "Let their table become a snare and a trap, And a stumbling block and a retribution to them.

> [10] "Let their eyes be darkened to see not, And bend their backs forever."

God has not failed, He has saved His people. Those who have come to him by faith in Christ, these are His people and they are saved. Those who have rejected Jesus will, as the Word promises, be rejected and lost forever.

The next question is, "Does this mean that there is no hope for the Jews?"

> [11] I say then, they did not stumble so as to fall, did they? May it never be! But by their transgression salvation has come to the Gentiles, to make them jealous.

Paul responds by saying that God uses their (the Jews who disbelieve) failure, not to annihilate them, but to bring others to salvation and to motivate them to belief. When the Jews themselves respond, it glorifies God because the promise then goes full circle (Jew to Gentile to Jew). Paul also uses this section to warn the Gentiles, who accepted the gospel, not to use this as a reason to boast or despise the Jews.

> [20] Quite right, they were broken off for their unbelief, but you stand by your faith. Do not be conceited, but fear; [21] for if God did not spare the natural branches, He will not spare you, either.

Verses 25-32 reveal a prophecy. The Jews, as a nation, will not all be destroyed and disappear. They will continue until the end of time:

- "Fullness of Gentiles" refers to the end of time when the last person will be saved and Jesus returns.
- The Jews will continue until the end, unlike other nations who come and go with time (e.g. Babylonians, Zoroastrians, etc.)

Paul continues his discussion about the end result of the Jewish people by stating that a part of them will never believe. This partial hardening is of the nation, not the individual. This is the result of their own disbelief from generation to generation until this very day. But in every generation some of them will believe, thus fulfilling God's Word about them, that He would save them.

> 25 For I do not want you, brethren, to be uninformed of this mystery—so that you will not be wise in your own estimation—that a partial hardening has happened to Israel until the fullness of the Gentiles has come in; 26 and so all Israel will be saved; just as it is written, "The Deliverer will come from Zion, He will remove ungodliness from Jacob."
> 27 "This is My covenant with them, When I take away their sins."

The term "all Israel" is not a reference to the cultural state of Israel but the spiritual Israel which is made up of those Jews who receive Christ (Romans 9:8).

Many use this passage to maintain a doctrine that says that all Jews will be saved eventually (contained in pre-millennial theory), but this violates every other Scripture about salvation and how it is obtained.

Paul says, God's Word has not failed the Jews:

- They were chosen and believed, and consequently, blessed as promised.
- They were first to receive the promise: Jesus was a Jew.
- Those who received it by faith were saved.

He also warns the Gentiles to be careful about their attitude towards the Jews since:

- It was Gentile unbelief that caused God to create the Jewish race through Abraham.

- It was Jewish unbelief that helped spread the gospel to the Gentiles.

- It is through Gentile belief that the gospel is now being spread to the Jews. Christ's Word is being spread by Gentiles, not Jews.

In this way both Jew and Gentile see their need for each other, and God uses both to save the other.

> 33 Oh, the depth of the riches both of the wisdom and knowledge of God! How unsearchable are His judgments and unfathomable His ways! 34 For who has known the mind of the Lord, or who became His counselor? 35 Or who has first given to Him that it might be paid back to him again? 36 For from Him and through Him and to Him are all things. To Him be the glory forever. Amen.

Paul finishes with a doxology (sudden outpouring) of praise for the way God has woven all of these things together to accomplish His purpose.

SUMMARY

The question was, "Why did Jews fail to obtain salvation/grace? Did the Law (Word) fail them?"

- Paul demonstrates that God's Word has never failed and He gives examples of this.

- He explains that the Jews failed to receive the promise because they tried to obtain it by works and not by faith.

- He shows that God's Word has always taught that faith is the basis by which man receives God's promises, both in the Old Testament and New Testament.

- He also shows that the Jews never responded properly to the Word and this fact was predicted by the Word.

- He explains that even though the Jews, in general, failed to receive the promise, God's Word did not fail because it said that:
    - The Jews would continue until the end of time, and they will (although mostly in disbelief).
    - He will save a remnant. In every generation some Jews believe in Jesus and are saved thus fulfilling God's Word.

For the Jewish people, the refusal of God's grace led to destruction, but in every age those who accept His grace through faith in Christ will receive salvation.

13.
The Result of Grace

ROMANS 12-16

In Romans 12:1-2, Paul makes a summary statement.

> 1 Therefore I urge you, brethren, by the mercies of God, to present your bodies a living and holy sacrifice, acceptable to God, which is your spiritual service of worship. 2 And do not be conformed to this world, but be transformed by the renewing of your mind, so that you may prove what the will of God is, that which is good and acceptable and perfect.

In essence he is saying, "If all that I have said is true, therefore, you should respond in the following way. Become living sacrifices. If God's grace has justified you from your sins and provided the Holy Spirit to enable you to be transformed by the process of sanctification, then your response is to manifest the work of God's grace through the Holy Spirit in your every day lives."

In the final chapter of this book I will summarize the instructions that Paul gives to his readers based on what he has taught them about the grace of God in the first 11 chapters of his book. Essentially, Romans 12-16 contain a description of what the transformation he talks about in Romans 12:1-2 is supposed to look like. It is the nuts and bolts of every day sanctified living. He mentions three basic virtues that encompass the sum of the sanctified life lived by those who have been transformed through the grace of God, the topic upon which this book is based ("Grace in the Book of Romans").

- Humility
- Love of other
- Submission

Those who live the sanctified life are the final result of grace, and when these people come together to worship God they are referred to as the Church of Christ (Romans 16:16).

MARKS OF TRANSFORMATION

If everything that Paul says is true, then our lives should bear the marks of **transformation**, the first being humility.

1. Humility - Romans 12:3-8

> 3 For through the grace given to me I say to everyone among you not to think more highly of himself than he ought to think; but to think so as to have sound judgment, as God has allotted to each a measure of faith. 4 For just as we have many members in one body and all the members do not have the same function, 5 so we, who are many, are one body in Christ, and individually members one of another. 6 Since we have gifts that differ according to the grace given to us, each of us is to exercise them accordingly: if prophecy, according to the proportion of his faith; 7 if service, in his serving; or he who teaches, in his teaching; 8 or he who exhorts, in his exhortation; he who gives, with liberality; he who leads, with diligence; he who shows mercy, with cheerfulness.

Some think that a humble person is one who is shy, speaks softly or has a passive nature, but in this passage Paul describes the truly humble person as one who has an accurate assessment of himself, not less or more. Humility enables a person to say "thank you" when complimented and "I am sorry" when in error. Humility is demonstrated through service not shyness.

The point Paul is making is that our transformation moves us towards humility of mind (accurate vision of self) and humility of actions (the use of our gifts and talents in the service of others rather than self). The fleshly, proud man will use his talents to serve his ego, comfort, security, goals and to "build bigger barns." The transformed man seeks to multiply his talents in the building of the kingdom, not his own house. Humility is the first mark of transformation.

2. Love - Romans 12:9-31

The second mark of transformation is love. In this passage Paul describes some facets of the kind of love that evidences a legitimate transformation. He mentions seven marks:

A. Sincere

> 9a Let love be without hypocrisy.

Not a show of love, but real love, felt love, sincere, loyal and pure love. Not sexual, social or family love, but sacrificial love that will pay a price for the other. The kind of love that goes to a cross for a friend, not double crosses a friend.

B. Pure

> 9b Abhor what is evil; cling to what is good.

A love that is high and noble and pure and right. A love that seeks the good for the other.

C. Edifying

> 10 Be devoted to one another in brotherly love; give preference to one another in honor; 11 not lagging behind in diligence, fervent in spirit, serving the Lord; 12 rejoicing in hope, persevering in tribulation, devoted to

> prayer, [13] contributing to the needs of the saints, practicing hospitality.

This love builds everything and everyone it touches. It esteems and builds the brethren it loves. It works hard in serving in the kingdom, and perseveres in both good and bad times (fervent in the Spirit).

D. Gracious

> [14] Bless those who persecute you; bless and do not curse.

A love that is willing to overlook an offence and is not easily provoked. It deflects criticism and gives the benefit of the doubt.

E. Empathetic

> [15] Rejoice with those who rejoice, and weep with those who weep.

This love not only feels the other's pain but shares the other's pain and joy. It is not afraid to get involved in someone else's life. True involvement is not meddling, but a willingness to listen and care.

F. Meek

> [16] Be of the same mind toward one another; do not be haughty in mind, but associate with the lowly. Do not be wise in your own estimation.

Humility is an accurate view of self. Meekness is the absence of the need to have one's own way all of the time. Being of the same mind means compromise, it means giving up one's will in order to create unity. The willingness to do it the other guy's way in order to build him up, this is meekness. We must not compromise truth and goodness, but most division in families and in churches occurs because one person or group wants its own way (usually because one thinks their way is best). We can have all the outward markings of the true church but if there is no meekness within we are like the Pharisees, concerned with externals and not truly transformed.

G. Peaceful

The work of the saved is reconciliation. We are ambassadors for Christ to an estranged world. In a war, ambassadors do not fight. Love in a transformed heart is peaceful and actively seeks peace with others ("Blessed are the peacemakers for they shall be called sons of God." Matthew 5:9). Paul explains not only the peaceful quality of transformed love, but also how one arrives here.

> 17a Never pay back evil for evil to anyone.

Deny yourself the pleasure of revenge.

> 17b Respect what is right in the sight of all men.

Respect what is right. You can protect yourself, stand up for what is right, use what is right to achieve justice and goodness, but do not return evil for evil.

> 18 If possible, so far as it depends on you, be at peace with all men. 19 Never take your own revenge, beloved, but leave room for the wrath of God, for it is written, "Vengeance is Mine, I will repay," says the Lord. 20" But if your enemy is hungry, feed him, and if he is thirsty, give him a drink; for in so doing you will heap burning coals on his head."

Seek the peaceful way as a solution. This can be costly and seem like a disadvantage at times, but Paul reassures us that God will meet out justice in the end. This is His promise so we should not worry.

> 21 Do not be overcome by evil, but overcome evil with good.

Do not revert back to the actions and methods that you used in your old life, allow the "transformed" man to respond. Let grace work, not sin.

3. Submission – Romans 13-14

In chapters 13 and 14 Paul goes on to talk about the third mark of a transformed life: submission. An attitude of submission is the ability to recognize and accept authority. Whether it be the authority of a person or a system, or merely the authority imposed on us by a set of circumstances, the Christian is able to recognize and submit to authority in all of its forms.

This is an obvious and central trait of the one who knows God and His grace. If one truly knows God (has an appreciation and understanding of this being called God) and not merely knows "about" God (academic knowledge), submission is a natural reaction. In the Old Testament whenever God manifested Himself, men fell on their faces in submission and worship. There was no bargaining on their part, they went into immediate submission.

Those who say they belong to God's kingdom and are Christ's disciples are claiming that they know God in Christ, and if they do they must learn submission because that is man's place in his relationship with God (Muslims have this idea as the core of their religion: the term Islam means surrender).

Submissiveness does not come naturally, we have to learn it (even Jesus learned about submission through the confining nature of His humanity and through the things He suffered because of it). As God, He did not have to obey, but as man He did. We also learn about this submissive attitude of spirit through various avenues, and this is what Paul describes here:

Submission to General Authority

> 1 Every person is to be in subjection to the governing
> authorities. For there is no authority except from God, and
> those which exist are established by God. 2 Therefore whoever
> resists authority has opposed the ordinance of God; and they
> who have opposed will receive condemnation upon
> themselves. 3 For rulers are not a cause of fear for good

> behavior, but for evil. Do you want to have no fear of authority? Do what is good and you will have praise from the same; [4] for it is a minister of God to you for good. But if you do what is evil, be afraid; for it does not bear the sword for nothing; for it is a minister of God, an avenger who brings wrath on the one who practices evil. [5] Therefore it is necessary to be in subjection, not only because of wrath, but also for conscience' sake. [6] For because of this you also pay taxes, for rulers are servants of God, devoting themselves to this very thing. [7] Render to all what is due them: tax to whom tax is due; custom to whom custom; fear to whom fear; honor to whom honor.

Paul lived at a time when the most ruthless world government reigned and yet explained that the attitude of Christians towards government in general was submissiveness. The role of Christians in this world is not to promote the kingdom of men, but to establish and maintain the kingdom of God. Rome fell without the political intervention of Christians, the kingdom of God eventually overtook it, as it will all other kingdoms that man establishes (Daniel 2:24-45).

Christians can be involved in politics, but only if they remember that they serve in the political arena as ambassadors for Christ. Their loyalty is to a higher government. All government should submit to God's authority and those who do not, God will depose in His time and manner. Christians show the work of the Spirit within themselves in that they recognize the true nature of government in God's plan and respond to it with this understanding.

Submission to Neighbors (Respect)

> [8] Owe nothing to anyone except to love one another; for he who loves his neighbor has fulfilled the law. [9] For this, "You shall not commit adultery, You shall not murder, You shall not steal, You shall not covet," and if there is any other commandment, it is summed up in this saying, "You shall love your neighbor as yourself." [10] Love does no wrong to a

> neighbor; therefore love is the fulfillment of the law. [11] Do this, knowing the time, that it is already the hour for you to awaken from sleep; for now salvation is nearer to us than when we believed. [12] The night is almost gone, and the day is near. Therefore let us lay aside the deeds of darkness and put on the armor of light. [13] Let us behave properly as in the day, not in carousing and drunkenness, not in sexual promiscuity and sensuality, not in strife and jealousy. [14] But put on the Lord Jesus Christ, and make no provision for the flesh in regard to its lusts.

One who is in submission to God and the government respects the society created by God and overseen by government.

Verses 8-10 summarize the attitude of the Christian in regard to society in general. The Old Testament Law regulated every form of conduct in regards to treatment of others within that society. Paul reduces all these regulations to one single command: love your neighbor. The Christian's submissive nature is seen in his attitude of love towards society in general. He lives by the rules of love to create an environment which promotes peace, respect and goodness in society including family.

Submission to Brethren (Regard)

> [1] Now accept the one who is weak in faith, but not for the purpose of passing judgment on his opinions. [2] One person has faith that he may eat all things, but he who is weak eats vegetables only. [3] The one who eats is not to regard with contempt the one who does not eat, and the one who does not eat is not to judge the one who eats, for God has accepted him. [4] Who are you to judge the servant of another? To his own master he stands or falls; and he will stand, for the Lord is able to make him stand. [5] One person regards one day above another, another regards every day alike. Each person must be fully convinced in his own mind. [6] He who observes the day, observes it for the Lord, and he who eats, does so for the Lord, for he gives thanks to God; and he who eats not, for the

Lord he does not eat, and gives thanks to God. 7 For not one of us lives for himself, and not one dies for himself; 8 for if we live, we live for the Lord, or if we die, we die for the Lord; therefore whether we live or die, we are the Lord's. 9 For to this end Christ died and lived again, that He might be Lord both of the dead and of the living. 10 But you, why do you judge your brother? Or you again, why do you regard your brother with contempt? For we will all stand before the judgment seat of God. 11 For it is written, "As I live, says the Lord, every knee shall bow to Me, And every tongue shall give praise to God." 12 So then each one of us will give an account of himself to God. 13 Therefore let us not judge one another anymore, but rather determine this—not to put an obstacle or a stumbling block in a brother's way. 14 I know and am convinced in the Lord Jesus that nothing is unclean in itself; but to him who thinks anything to be unclean, to him it is unclean. 15 For if because of food your brother is hurt, you are no longer walking according to love. Do not destroy with your food him for whom Christ died. 16 Therefore do not let what is for you a good thing be spoken of as evil; 17 for the kingdom of God is not eating and drinking, but righteousness and peace and joy in the Holy Spirit. 18 For he who in this way serves Christ is acceptable to God and approved by men. 19 So then we pursue the things which make for peace and the building up of one another. 20 Do not tear down the work of God for the sake of food. All things indeed are clean, but they are evil for the man who eats and gives offense. 21 It is good not to eat meat or to drink wine, or to do anything by which your brother stumbles. 22 The faith which you have, have as your own conviction before God. Happy is he who does not condemn himself in what he approves. 23 But he who doubts is condemned if he eats, because his eating is not from faith; and whatever is not from faith is sin.

1 Now we who are strong ought to bear the weaknesses of those without strength and not just please ourselves. 2 Each of us is to please his neighbor for his good, to his edification. 3 For even Christ did not please Himself; but as it is written,

> "The reproaches of those who reproached You fell on Me."
> 4 For whatever was written in earlier times was written for
> our instruction, so that through perseverance and the
> encouragement of the Scriptures we might have hope. 5 Now
> may the God who gives perseverance and encouragement
> grant you to be of the same mind with one another according
> to Christ Jesus, 6 so that with one accord you may with one
> voice glorify the God and Father of our Lord Jesus Christ.
> 7 Therefore, accept one another, just as Christ also accepted us
> to the glory of God. 8 For I say that Christ has become a
> servant to the circumcision on behalf of the truth of God to
> confirm the promises given to the fathers, 9 and for the
> Gentiles to glorify God for His mercy; as it is written,
> "Therefore I will give praise to You among the Gentiles, And I
> will sing to Your name." 10 Again he says, "Rejoice, O Gentiles,
> with His people." 11 And again, "Praise the Lord all you
> Gentiles, And let all the peoples praise Him." 12 Again Isaiah
> says, "There shall come the root of Jesse, And He who arises to
> rule over the Gentiles, In Him shall the Gentiles hope." 13 Now
> may the God of hope fill you with all joy and peace in
> believing, so that you will abound in hope by the power of the
> Holy Spirit.

Paul closes the circle (government/society, family/church). Your family is not necessarily your brethren, but your brethren will always be your family. In the last few chapters he describes the submissive attitude that needs to exist between brethren as a mark that they are both born of the same Spirit. The key verse is 15:7:

> 7 Therefore, accept one another, just as Christ also accepted us to the glory of God.

The issue at the time was the fact that some, who were more confident in the grace of Christ, permitted themselves certain things (e.g. the eating of meats once used in pagan rituals) which in itself was not wrong, but which others (less confident in that grace) did not. Conflict arose because those who had the confidence to eat without guilt became impatient with the fear and uncertainty of those who could not partake because of a weak conscience. This impatience demonstrated itself in unkindness (passing judgment on the "immaturity" of the weak; "What is his problem?"). The weak, on the other hand, seized the opportunity to criticize and condemn others who participated in something that they would not themselves do because of conscience, not the Lord's command. The result was division and isolation brought on by pride, lack of love and failure to submit.

Paul tells them to measure their attitude towards each other against Christ's attitude toward them: acceptance. The strongest of all did not judge us in our weakness. He became weak in order to save the weak.

Mutual submission in Christ sees the strong becoming weak in order to help the weak grow strong so all can be powerful in Christ and thus glorify God.

FINAL EXHORTATIONS

After describing the three manifestations of a life dedicated to God (humility, love and submission) Paul completes his letter with final greetings and exhortations to people he knows in the church.

Just Do It! - Romans 15:14-21

Listen carefully to what he has preached, respond to it and encourage each other to do so as well.

My own message to you, the reader, is the same. You may not understand or agree with everything in this book, but you should respond in obedience to what you do understand and what you agree is from God.

The only way grace begins its work is when we respond to God in obedience (Romans 1:17-18).

Pray - Romans 15:22-33

Paul asked them to pray for his ministry and that he might be with them in his travels.

I also ask for your prayers that God bless my own service of preaching and teaching through the BibleTalk.tv ministry.

Greetings and Praise - Romans 16:1-27

Paul has a series of personal greetings full of affection and encouragement. He warns them to be careful regarding false teachers and how to deal with them (point them out and turn them out). He finishes with a final word of praise to God for having revealed the way by which all men can be saved: a salvation offered by His grace and received through our faith in Jesus Christ expressed in repentance and baptism.

I also finish by thanking you for reading this book and hope that it has blessed you in some way. I leave you with the reminder that in the end, all I can do is explain to an extent His kindness, mercy and love, but only God is worthy of praise in Jesus' name. Amen.

BIBLETALK.TV IS AN INTERNET MISSION WORK.

We provide video and textual Bible teaching material on our website and mobile apps for free. We enable churches and individuals all over the world to have access to high quality Bible materials for personal growth, group study or for teaching in their classes.

The goal of this mission work is to spread the gospel to the greatest number of people using the latest technology available. For the first time in history it is becoming possible to preach the gospel to the entire world at once. BibleTalk.tv is an effort to preach the gospel to all nations every day until Jesus returns.

The Choctaw Church of Christ in Oklahoma City is the sponsoring congregation for this work and provides the oversight for the BibleTalk ministry team. If you would like information on how you can support this ministry, please go to the link provided below.

bibletalk.tv/support

Made in the USA
Monee, IL
18 October 2026

66036544R00069